100
THINGS TO
KNOW ABOUT
SPORTS

Usborne Quicklinks

For links to websites and videos where you
can watch world-class athletes break records,
test your sporting know-how with quizzes and
discover more about the facts described in this book,
go to **usborne.com/Quicklinks** and type in
the keywords: **things to know about sports**.

Here are some of the things you can do at the websites we recommend:

• Compare the speed of an Olympic sprinter with a cheetah.
• Watch an Olympic gymnast perform a medal-winning vault.
• See an accountant replace an injured goalie in an ice hockey match.
• Visit an island in Scotland where granite is quarried to make curling stones.

Please follow the online safety guidelines at Usborne Quicklinks.
Children should be supervised online.

100
THINGS TO
KNOW ABOUT
SPORTS

Written by
Alice James, Jerome Martin, Tom Mumbray and Micaela Tapsell

Illustrated by
Federico Mariani, Dominique Byron,
Parko Polo, Anton Hallmann and Jake Williams

Designed by
Jenny Offley, Lenka Jones,
Lizzie Knott and Jenny Hastings

1 Dancing is a sport...

but croquet isn't.

People have invented countless competitive games and activities, from discus-throwing to dominoes to dodgeball.
But what is a **sport**, and what *isn't*?

SPORTS SORTING MACHINE

There's no *one* thing that makes a sport a sport.
To be defined as a sport, most people agree an activity must pass a series of tests. Follow this machine around to find out what makes something a sport — and what doesn't count.

START HERE

1
Does it require
physical effort?
For example, can you get better at it by building up your strength or fitness?

YES

NO

YES

2
Does it require
physical skill?
Can you get better at it by improving your skills, agility and technique?

NO

Activities have to pass *all* five of these tests to be considered sports. But the criteria and definitions can change — sometimes people disagree.

3

Does it have
rules to follow?
Are they clear and agreed
upon by all who participate
in the activity?

YES →

NO ↓

4

Does it involve
competition
with other athletes?
Is it possible to win or
lose, or measure success?

NO

YES ↓

5

Is it
fun to watch?
Will it inspire people and
attract spectators to
stadiums and competitions?

NO ←

YES ↓

NOT A SPORT

HORSE LONG JUMP

CROQUET

TUG-OF-WAR

In **croquet** players hit
balls through hoops on
a lawn. It featured in
the 1900 Olympics, but
was discontinued when
only a single person
showed up to watch.

A SPORT

DARTS

DIVING

DANCING

Breaking or **break
dancing** is a style
of street dance born
from hip-hop music.
Competitions feature
athletic moves and
complicated techniques.

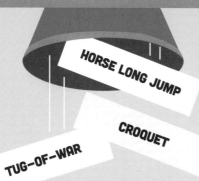

2 The athlete who runs furthest...

isn't even in the competition.

In the course of a game, players in different sports can cover a surprising amount of ground. But soccer referees frequently outrun them all.

This graph compares the average distances covered, in a single match or game, by athletes in various popular sports. Players in some positions tend to run more, while others, such as soccer goalkeepers, don't move as much.

Tennis players cover a big range of distances. Games can last anywhere from under 60 minutes to over 10 hours.

This is the distance run by a netball player in center position. The court is small — but players change direction once every four seconds, for the whole 60-minute game.

THWACK

BOING

TENNIS PLAYER	BASKETBALL PLAYER	NETBALL PLAYER	RUGBY PLAYER
2.5 miles (4km)	2 miles (3km)	5 miles (8km)	4.5 miles (7km)

Soccer players run a long way because games are long, the field is big, and players usually stay on for the majority of the game.

But soccer referees run *even* further. They have to keep within 20 yards (18m) of the player with the ball – which means they run further than any player.

To make sure they can keep up with the demands of a full game, referees have to take regular fitness tests.

WHOOSH

OOF

Let's take a moment to appreciate the referee who's made all the tough calls today while outrunning every player on the field!

FOOTBALL PLAYER	SOCCER PLAYER	SOCCER REFEREE	
1.25 miles (2km)	6 miles (10km)	7.5 miles (12km)	

3 Cheetahs and para-sprinters...

both run on springs.

The fastest para-sprinters, runners with one or no lower limbs, can race 100m in 10 seconds using high-tech **running blades**. The designers of the blades took inspiration from the world's fastest land animal: the cheetah.

The secret to a cheetah's speed is the way it can bend and flex its powerful, springy hind legs. The shape of the blades is designed to do the same.

Each blade functions like a spring that propels the athlete forward with maximum power.

The blades are made from up to 90 sheets of carbon, each thinner than a human hair, fused together. This makes the blades strong and light, allowing the runner to reach top speeds.

4 A bunch of celery leaves...

marked an athlete's crowning achievement.

The Ancient Greeks held four big sports competitions, known together as the **Panhellenic Games**. The winners weren't presented with bronze, silver or gold, but with **wreaths** made from different leaves.

Olympic Games

Olive wreath

The very first Olympics involved just one event – a race called the **stadio**. Events were added over time, including wrestling, boxing and chariot racing.

Pythian Games

Laurel wreath

The Pythian Games started out as a music contest. Sports events were added later.

Isthmian Games

Pine wreath

The Isthmian Games featured sports, but also poetry.

Some winners were given a poem called an ode instead of a wreath.

Nemean Games

Wild celery wreath

Initially only top athletes competed in these games, but later the games were opened to anyone who wanted to take part.

The Ancient Olympic Games began more than 2,800 years ago in 776 BCE. They were held every four years for around a thousand years, but then stopped.

In 1896 the games were revived, and the modern Olympic Games as we know them today began.

5 More than 300 events...

are contested in the Olympic Games.

The first modern Olympic Games were held in Athens in 1896. There were just 200 competitors, and nine sports. Today there are more than 300 events, and each Games is different to the last.

Today there are around 30 sports, but that doesn't mean athletes can only compete in 30 events. Each sport is broken down like this:

SPORTS

In the Olympics, "sports" is a broad category. It's defined as a group with one international governing body.

For example, **aquatics** is an Olympic sport.

DISCIPLINES

Sports are broken down into disciplines. Usually, an athlete will only compete in one discipline.

There are five aquatic disciplines: **swimming**, **open water swimming**, **diving**, **synchronized swimming** and **water polo**.

EVENTS

Within each discipline there are different events. An event is a competition in which you can win a medal. Athletes often compete in more than one.

Within swimming there are 32 events – for example **100m backstroke**.

THE FIRST MODERN OLYMPICS

These nine sports were included in the first modern Olympics.

Athletics

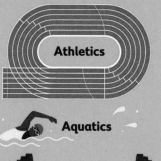

Aquatics

Weightlifting

Fencing

The Summer Olympics are held every four years. There are only five sports that have been included in *every* Summer Olympics since they started: **athletics**, **aquatics**, **cycling**, **fencing** and **gymnastics**.

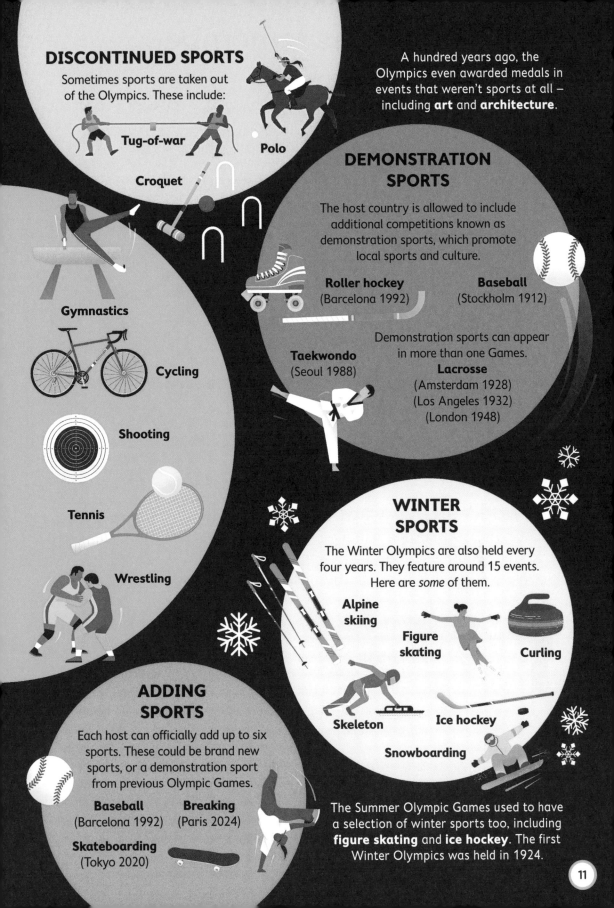

DISCONTINUED SPORTS

Sometimes sports are taken out of the Olympics. These include:

Tug-of-war

Polo

Croquet

A hundred years ago, the Olympics even awarded medals in events that weren't sports at all – including **art** and **architecture**.

DEMONSTRATION SPORTS

The host country is allowed to include additional competitions known as demonstration sports, which promote local sports and culture.

Roller hockey
(Barcelona 1992)

Baseball
(Stockholm 1912)

Demonstration sports can appear in more than one Games.

Taekwondo
(Seoul 1988)

Lacrosse
(Amsterdam 1928)
(Los Angeles 1932)
(London 1948)

Gymnastics

Cycling

Shooting

Tennis

Wrestling

WINTER SPORTS

The Winter Olympics are also held every four years. They feature around 15 events. Here are *some* of them.

Alpine skiing

Figure skating

Curling

Skeleton

Ice hockey

Snowboarding

ADDING SPORTS

Each host can officially add up to six sports. These could be brand new sports, or a demonstration sport from previous Olympic Games.

Baseball
(Barcelona 1992)

Breaking
(Paris 2024)

Skateboarding
(Tokyo 2020)

The Summer Olympic Games used to have a selection of winter sports too, including **figure skating** and **ice hockey**. The first Winter Olympics was held in 1924.

6 Your muscles remember...

tricky twists and turns.

Gymnast Simone Biles takes just five seconds to perform moves on the vault that are so difficult they were once considered impossible. To get her signature moves right at such high speeds, she relies on something called **muscle memory**.

By repeating her moves over and over in training, Biles strengthens the pathways in her brain that instruct her body what to do.

Here's a breakdown of those instructions:

- Run an exact number of steps
- Lunge for momentum
- Spot the springboard
- Swing arms to accelerate
- Push off from dominant leg
- Point toes

7 Gymnasts have one move...

that works on *every* apparatus.

Artistic gymnasts compete in a range of events, performing routines on different apparatuses. But only one move is used on them all: the **handstand**.

UNEVEN BARS

Gymnasts hold a handstand position before swinging around the bar in a move called a **giant**.

Hand guards and chalk help gymnasts grip the bars as they swing.

Women's apparatus events: vault, beam, uneven bars and floor

Men's apparatus events: vault, high bar, parallel bars, floor, rings and pommel horse

PARALLEL BARS

To perform a handstand pirouette, gymnasts move both hands across to a single bar in order to turn around.

During a routine, gymnasts' feet are not allowed to touch the floor.

Eventually, Biles is able to perform the skill automatically, without thinking. Scientists call this motor learning, or muscle memory.

Whatever their sport, any athlete who wants to perform with speed and precision, without having to think about every move, must build muscle memory – just like Biles.

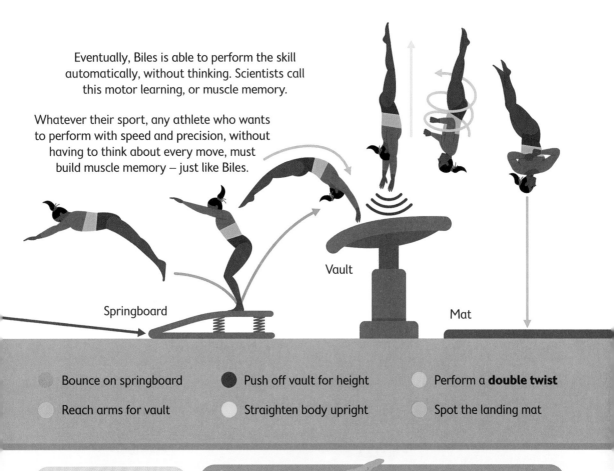

Vault

Springboard

Mat

- Bounce on springboard
- Reach arms for vault
- Push off vault for height
- Straighten body upright
- Perform a **double twist**
- Spot the landing mat

RINGS

A routine on the rings typically includes a swing into a handstand. Gymnasts use the muscles in their core and arms to keep their bodies straight while hanging upside down.

BALANCE BEAM

Gymnasts pass through a handstand position, with their legs in splits, during a move called a **backwards walkover**.

Beam dimensions: 16ft (5m) long, 4in (10cm) wide – the same width as this box.

FLOOR

This move is called a Japanese handstand. Gymnasts must hold the position for at least 2 seconds.

Springs under the floor help propel gymnasts into tumbles and absorb the impact when they land.

SCORING POINTS

Before competitions, each gymnast is given a **difficulty score** – the harder their routine, the higher their score. Points are deducted from their score for every error they make during their routine, such as a wobble or fall.

8 A curvy swimming pool...

made modern skateboarding possible.

In **vert**, or vertical skateboarding, skaters swoop up and down steep, curving ramps and do flips and spins high in the air. Many of those tricks might not exist today if it hadn't been for a particular swimming pool in Finland.

In the 1920s and '30s, the standard shape for swimming pools in people's backyards was a simple rectangle with a flat bottom and square corners.

Then, in 1939, a Finnish architect named Alvar Aalto designed a new pool for a fashionable villa.

It was rounded all over, with swooping curves leading into bowl-shaped ends.

The pool was an instant hit. People copied the design in *thousands* of backyards around the world.

Then, in the 1970s, a drought struck California. People had to save as much water as they could, so many emptied their pools.

Groups of young skateboarders spotted these empty pools and they had a bright — if illegal — idea.

They began sneaking into people's backyards to skate *in their pools*.

They found that by skating on the curving slopes of Aalto's pool, they could pick up lots of speed...

...and could even skate *up* the sides and fly into the air. This is how vert skateboarding was invented.

Aw, this is rad!

Dude, go tell everybody they've *got* to see this!

Today, the bowls, curves and steep slopes of that Finnish pool can be found in skate parks all around the globe.

15

9 Huddles helped to hide...

secret sign language.

In 1892, a team of deaf students was playing a game of football. They were using sign language to discuss tactics, when they had an idea that changed the sport forever.

The team's captain, Paul Hubbard, noticed that players on the other team were looking at his sign language to figure out his game plan.

He asked his teammates to form a circle around him to cover his signs and keep their strategies secret. In doing so, they formed the first team huddle.

Today, athletes of all abilities use the huddle in lots of different sports, to motivate, strategize and celebrate as a team.

10 Cherry pies and UFOs...

combined to create the ultimate game.

Ultimate is a team sport in which players race up and down a pitch, passing and catching a flying disc called a frisbee to score points. These days, the disc is made of plastic – but it didn't start out that way.

People were throwing dishes, lids, pans and other flat discs through the air long before ultimate existed... but it took a few key innovations to transform this quirky pastime into a sport.

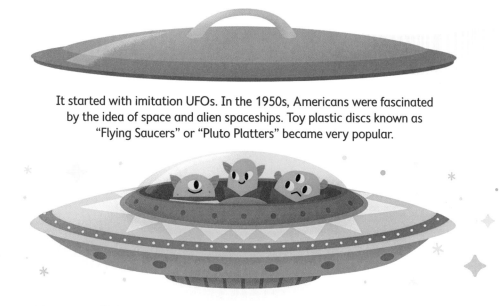

It started with imitation UFOs. In the 1950s, Americans were fascinated by the idea of space and alien spaceships. Toy plastic discs known as "Flying Saucers" or "Pluto Platters" became very popular.

Then, in the 1960s, college students tossed back and forth empty fruit pie dishes from their dining halls. They invented a new game and called it ultimate.

The game became so popular that sturdier, better-balanced plastic discs were developed.

With these new discs, the fast-paced sport of ultimate really took off. Today, it's played by over 7 million people in over 80 countries.

11 Hundreds of dimples...

make a golf ball fly further.

Balls for different sports are designed with different situations in mind. Here are some examples, drawn to scale with each other.

GOLF

There are usually 300-600 dimples on a golf ball. These make it fly *twice* as far as it would if it were smooth.

The dimples make the air move quickly around the ball as it flies. This is called **turbulence**, and it reduces **drag** – the force that would slow a ball down.

SOFTBALL

A softball isn't actually soft. It's called softball because it's thrown at the person batting with an underarm throw – that's a soft throw from the waist.

HANDBALL

According to the rules of handball, the ball must have a non-slippery surface. Otherwise it would fall out of players' hands.

In fact, top handball players even rub a sticky resin on to their balls, to help them grip.

SQUELCH

BADMINTON

Shuttlecocks are traditionally made with goose feathers. But only the feathers from one wing are used, not a mix of both, or they wouldn't fly evenly.

There are exactly 16 feathers in every shuttlecock.

BASKETBALL

The balls used in professional games are all made by the same brand. They each have a lifespan of **10,000** bounces.

SQUASH

Made from bouncy rubber, squash balls have different dots to indicate how bouncy they are.

Balls with two yellow dots are the LEAST bouncy. They're used in professional matches.

Balls with a blue dot bounce the highest, so they're easier to play with.

During a game, the rubber ball heats up as it is hit around. The hotter it gets, the bouncier it is.

SHOT

This is the heaviest ball in any sport, weighing **15lb (7kg)** or more. In competitions athletes need a lot of strength and speed to throw – or **put** – the shot as far as possible.

Sports historians think that the first shots were probably rocks or cannonballs.

TENNIS

Nitrogen gas is injected into tennis balls to inflate them. They are inflated an *exact* amount, so when they're dropped they have *just* the right bounce.

12 Standing still...

is the best way to save a penalty in soccer.

A penalty is a single kick that could mean the difference between winning or losing. As the striker approaches the ball, the goalkeeper must decide which way to dive – or whether to dive at all.

Strikers score penalties **75%** of the time. The odds are stacked against the goalie.

What should I do?

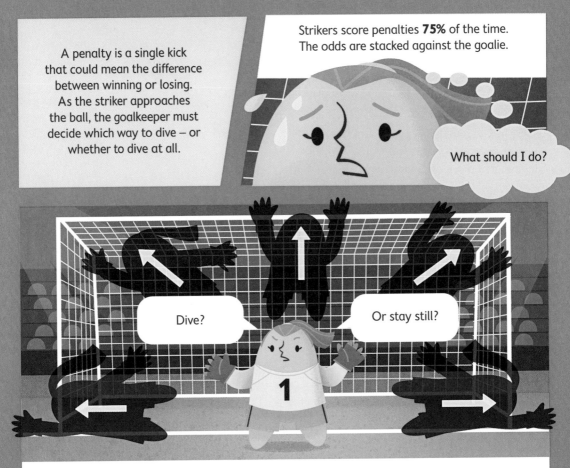

Dive?

Or stay still?

A goalie could jump up, or dive to any corner of the goal. And, usually, they do – even though statistics show that the best choice is actually to stay exactly where they are.

A goalie who stands still is **twice** as likely to save a penalty as one who dives.

HURRAH!

Even when goalkeepers know this, they often still dive. In fact, they dive **98%** of the time. This is because of something called **action bias**. It means that in a critical moment, a person would almost always rather do *something* than *nothing*.

13 A list of rules...

broke records at auction.

In 1891, a P.E. teacher created a new game to occupy his students during the winter. He typed out 13 rules. A century later this list was sold for *millions* of dollars, and the game had become one of the world's most popular sports: basketball.

In 2010, the original list was auctioned for **$4.3 million**.

It was the most expensive piece of sports memorabilia at that time.

Basket Ball

The ball to be an ordinary Association foot ball.
1. The ball may be thrown in any direction with one or both hands.
2. The ball may be batted in any direction with one or both hands (never with the fist).
3. The player cannot run with the ball, the player must throw it from the spot on which he catches it,

In 2022, basketball memorabilia broke records again when a jersey worn by player Michael Jordan sold for over **$10 million**.

FROM BASKETS TO HOOPS

In the original game, players scored goals by throwing the ball into peach baskets fixed to 10ft (3.05m) high balconies. This is still the basket height in all professional courts, although the wooden baskets have been replaced by metal hoops.

By the 1920s, there were hundreds of professional basketball teams across the United States.	There are now over **400 million** basketball players worldwide.

14 Sliders, slurves and splitters...

put batters in a spin.

To score points in baseball, a batter must start by hitting a ball thrown by a pitcher. It's the pitcher's job to make the ball fiendishly difficult for the batter to hit. So, pitchers spend years perfecting their throw to make the ball fly in unusual ways.

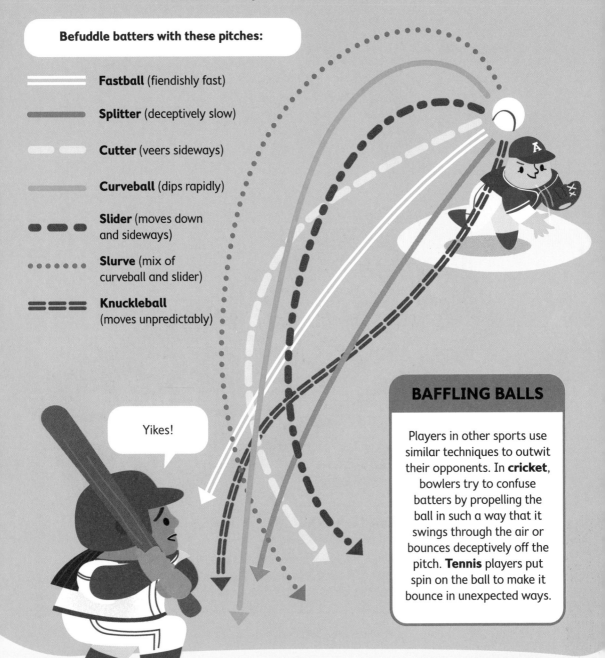

Befuddle batters with these pitches:

Fastball (fiendishly fast)

Splitter (deceptively slow)

Cutter (veers sideways)

Curveball (dips rapidly)

Slider (moves down and sideways)

Slurve (mix of curveball and slider)

Knuckleball (moves unpredictably)

Yikes!

BAFFLING BALLS

Players in other sports use similar techniques to outwit their opponents. In **cricket**, bowlers try to confuse batters by propelling the ball in such a way that it swings through the air or bounces deceptively off the pitch. **Tennis** players put spin on the ball to make it bounce in unexpected ways.

15 Picky pitchers...

go through a hundred baseballs a game.

Only one ball is in play at a time, but a typical professional game of baseball requires a hundred balls. So why are so many balls discarded in the course of a game?

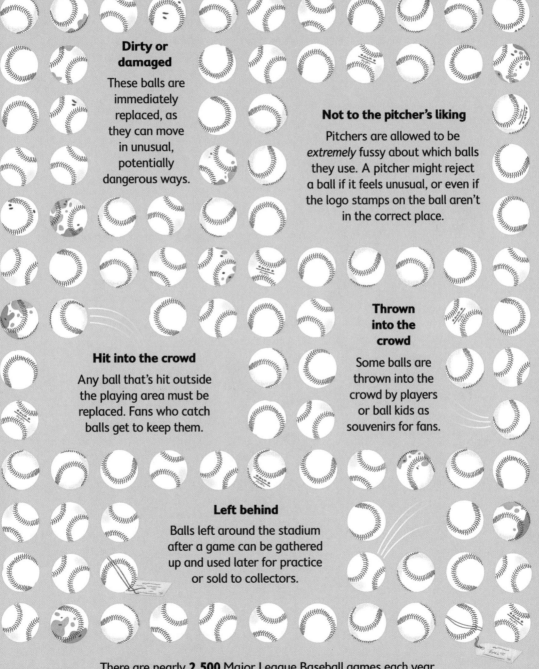

Dirty or damaged

These balls are immediately replaced, as they can move in unusual, potentially dangerous ways.

Not to the pitcher's liking

Pitchers are allowed to be *extremely* fussy about which balls they use. A pitcher might reject a ball if it feels unusual, or even if the logo stamps on the ball aren't in the correct place.

Hit into the crowd

Any ball that's hit outside the playing area must be replaced. Fans who catch balls get to keep them.

Thrown into the crowd

Some balls are thrown into the crowd by players or ball kids as souvenirs for fans.

Left behind

Balls left around the stadium after a game can be gathered up and used later for practice or sold to collectors.

There are nearly **2,500** Major League Baseball games each year, so more than a **quarter of a million** balls are used in total.

16 The perfect splash...

depends on what a diver does *underwater.*

In competitions, divers are judged on more than just dramatic flips, tucks and tumbles. Even the size of the splash they make is important: the smaller the splash, the higher the score. Divers can control this by maintaining the perfect body position as they enter the water – but the quest for a smaller splash *also* continues *below* the surface.

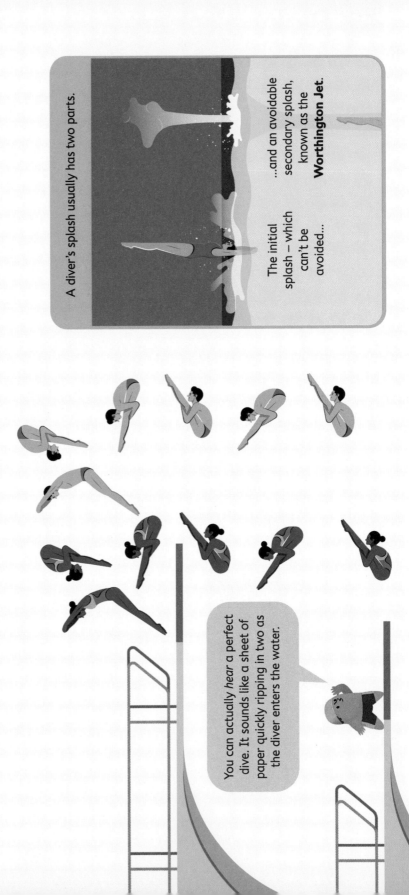

A diver's splash usually has two parts.

The initial splash – which can't be avoided...

...and an avoidable secondary splash, known as the **Worthington Jet.**

You can actually *hear* a perfect dive. It sounds like a sheet of paper quickly ripping in two as the diver enters the water.

These two divers both enter the water with the same perfect body position...

...but *this* diver has forgotten her training! She plunges straight down into the water, creating a large air pocket.

When the water rushes back in to fill that air pocket, it will force up a huge Worthington Jet.

This diver has remembered his training. So, as soon as he enters the water, he pushes his arms wide out to the side and does an underwater flip.

This breaks the air pocket around him into lots of tiny air bubbles.

If a diver knows how to move underwater, the secondary splash may be little more than a fizzing of tiny bubbles at the surface.

17 A woman in disguise...

proved race officials wrong.

Women haven't always been allowed to take part in the Boston marathon. Race officials used to believe they couldn't run such long distances – a marathon is 26 miles (42km) long. But in 1966, it took just one rule-breaking woman to make history.

On the morning of the marathon, Bobbi Gibb disguised herself as a man and hid in a bush, waiting for the race to start.

When the race gun sounded, Gibb leaped out to join the runners. The crowd cheered her on.

She finished the marathon in just three hours and twenty-one minutes – faster than two thirds of her male competitors.

In the years that followed, Gibb returned to run the marathon again, with more rule-breaking women by her side.

ABOUT THE BOSTON MARATHON

First held in 1897, the Boston Marathon is the world's oldest annual marathon.

The rule that banned women was finally lifted in 1972.

Today, around 10,000 female runners take part in the Boston Marathon every year.

18 People invented skiing...

long before they invented writing.

Thousands of years before writing was invented, people were already climbing, skiing, swimming and rowing. Although no one knows when these activities became sports, cave paintings from around the world have helped archeologists piece together sporting history.

Climbing

Cave location: Spain

Date: 8,000 years old

Paintings like these reveal an advanced knowledge of rope-climbing techniques.

Skiing

Cave location: China

Date: Between 10,000 and 30,000 years old

Some archeologists think this could be the oldest known example of skiing.

Swimming

Cave location: Egypt

Date: 10,000 years old

Found in the Cave of Swimmers, this painting could be the oldest known record of swimming.

Rowing

Cave location: Australia

Date: Up to 60,000 years old

This artwork shows how people first arrived in Australia — in boats similar to modern-day canoes.

19 To be the best in the world...

start with a watch and a plan.

Some athletes use gadgets that measure *every* aspect of their training, from how much power their legs produce to how much oxygen they're breathing out. Others become champions without gadgets.

With many gold medals and world records, Eliud Kipchoge is one of the best long-distance runners of all time. He lives and trains in Kenya, and keeps a very simple schedule.

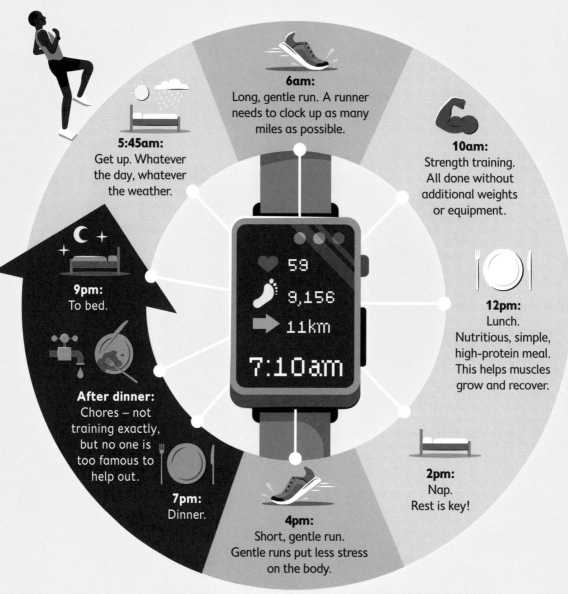

6am:
Long, gentle run. A runner needs to clock up as many miles as possible.

5:45am:
Get up. Whatever the day, whatever the weather.

10am:
Strength training. All done without additional weights or equipment.

9pm:
To bed.

59
9,156
11km
7:10am

12pm:
Lunch. Nutritious, simple, high-protein meal. This helps muscles grow and recover.

After dinner:
Chores – not training exactly, but no one is too famous to help out.

2pm:
Nap. Rest is key!

7pm:
Dinner.

4pm:
Short, gentle run. Gentle runs put less stress on the body.

Whatever sport an athlete trains for, and whatever style of training they choose, all training plans will include the same key elements: plenty of sleep, nutritious food for energy and muscle repair, and lots and lots of hard work.

20 Fast food on poles...

helps marathon swimmers across the line.

Marathon swimmers race over long distances, which uses enormous amounts of energy. This means they have to refuel on the move. They can't carry much, so the swimmers rely on an unusual delivery service.

Marathon swimmers compete in races that are at least **6.2 miles (10km)** long. Even the quickest races take a couple of hours to complete, so swimmers have to take on fuel.

There are floating feeding stations along the route, where coaches attach water bottles and little pouches filled with energy gel to the end of long poles. Then they dangle them out to their swimmers.

Swimmers have to spot their flag, grab their supplies, then roll onto their backs to gulp down the food or water before racing away.

All sorts of endurance athletes, from swimmers to cyclists to long-distance runners, face the problem of how to refuel during a competition. Finding the right solution can make the difference between victory and defeat.

21 To feel friendlier...

go for a jog.

When you do sports or exercise, even for a short time, it triggers a swirly rush of chemicals in your brain and all around your body. This can have big effects – including making you calmer, happier and even friendlier.

Here are some of the chemicals that increase in your brain while you're exercising:

NOREPINEPHRINE

This chemical helps you deal with stress and improves your mood and concentration.

SEROTONIN

This is a messenger in your brain that makes you feel less worried and more joyful.

OXYTOCIN

A type of chemical called a hormone. It makes you feel more trusting, loved and calm.

DOPAMINE

This feel-good hormone gives your brain a reward and makes you feel great.

We LOVE being part of this team.

You worked so hard!

Here's a prize for taking part!

22 Your body can trick you...

into racing faster.

You're on the starting line for the biggest race of your life.
The crowd is quiet and your nerves are shaking... Get ready... Set... GO!
When a race begins, a whole new chemical fires off – and it can lead
to the best performances of an athlete's life.

ADRENALINE

This hormone prepares your body for the most extreme situations, such as if you have to escape danger. These are some of the things it does inside your body...

Produce sweat! Cool this runner down!

Boost focus. This race is all that matters!

Turn off feelings of pain! These legs are starting to hurt and we don't want that slowing us down.

OFF   ON

PAIN SWITCH

Get that heart beating faster. We need as much oxygen in the muscles as possible.

OXYGEN

Digest sugars now! We need all the energy we can get.

When adrenaline wears off, the athlete feels completely exhausted.
But during a race, it can help athletes to achieve far more than they can in training.

23 An Icelandic legend...

tests the world's strongest athletes.

In a chilly corner of Iceland, around 200 years ago, a farmer used large stones to build a sheep pen. Legend tells that his daughter carried the biggest and heaviest of these stones all the way around the pen. And so began a tradition of strength challenges...

I am the famous **Húsafell Stone**. Lift me if you dare!

But let me warn you, I weigh 410 lb (186kg) and I'm particularly hard to grip.

Do you think you're strong enough?

Baaa

Baaaa

Since then, people have visited Iceland from far and wide in an attempt to lift the stone and prove their strength. Those who can move it from the ground are given titles:

Amlóði
(lazybones)

Those who can lift the stone only to their knees.

Sheesh... is that the best you can do? You're a lazybones!

Hálfsterkur
(half-strength)

Those who can lift the stone to their waist.

Ha! Not a bad attempt... you're a half-strength!

Fullsterkur
(full-strength)

Those who match the strength of the farmer's daughter by carrying the stone around the pen.

Agh! A full-strength! Put me down!

Elsewhere, replicas of the Húsafell stone are used in professional strength competitions around the world.

24 The biggest prize...

is sometimes the smallest trophy.

At least once every two years, England and Australia play a series of cricket matches called the **Ashes**. It's one of the biggest competitions in international cricket. But the trophy for the men's Ashes is smaller than your hand.

The Ashes trophy was made in the 1880s. According to one story, it contains the burned remains (the ashes) of cricket bails from a match between England and Australia.

In another story, it contains the ashes of an Australian bride's veil.

Bails

No one actually knows for sure what's inside. It may even contain nothing at all.

This is the real size of the trophy.

The entire competition is named after these famous, mysterious ashes.

The tiny trophy is made of terracotta — a type of clay.

This original trophy is kept at Lord's Cricket Ground in London. The winning team is awarded a replica.

Bails (life-size)

Professional gamers train...

ith the help of sports scientists.

ofessional gamers, called E-athletes, put their skills to the test in front
millions of spectators in elite gaming tournaments. But behind every
athlete is a team of experts and sports scientists who help them train.

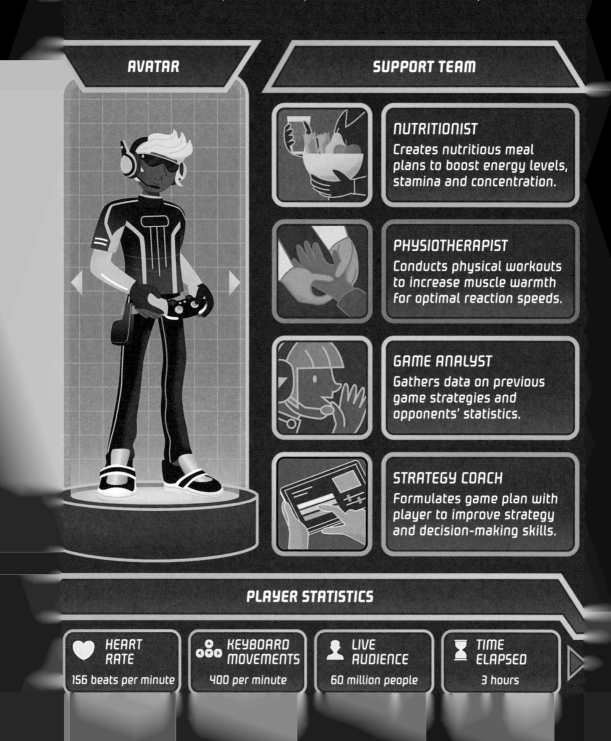

AVATAR

SUPPORT TEAM

NUTRITIONIST
Creates nutritious meal plans to boost energy levels, stamina and concentration.

PHYSIOTHERAPIST
Conducts physical workouts to increase muscle warmth for optimal reaction speeds.

GAME ANALYST
Gathers data on previous game strategies and opponents' statistics.

STRATEGY COACH
Formulates game plan with player to improve strategy and decision-making skills.

PLAYER STATISTICS

HEART RATE
156 beats per minute

KEYBOARD MOVEMENTS
400 per minute

LIVE AUDIENCE
60 million people

TIME ELAPSED
3 hours

26 Javelins flew *too* far...

until they were redesigned.

For thousands of years, athletes have thrown javelins further and further – until 1986, when the javelin had to be redesigned to stop this pattern of progress and keep spectators safe.

By the 1980s, professional athletes had become so good at throwing javelins that they were at risk of throwing them out of bounds, too close to spectators.

Wuh-oh! We're going to have to change these javelins to make them *less* aerodynamic!

So in 1986, engineers made the pointed tip of the javelin rounder and blunter and moved its weighted section nearly 2 inches (5cm) forward. This caused the nose of the javelin to tip down sooner during flight.

These changes had a significant effect, reducing throwing distances by 10% – keeping athletes, spectators and officials safe.

Flight path of original javelin

Redesigned javelin

27 Basketball battles...

are fought on super-reinforced wheels.

Bash, clash, SCREEEEECH. In the fast-paced game of wheelchair basketball, athletes jostle and scrap for the ball, then charge down the court to score goals, or block them. Players need tough chairs, carefully designed to withstand these fierce on-court battles.

The game is intense! We all speed around the court fighting for the ball, and it can get rough!

SCREECH

We're strapped in to make sure we don't fall out if our chairs rock.

Most chairs are made from aerospace-grade aluminum – the same metal used to build planes. That's how tough they need to be.

See the extra little wheels on the back? They stop our chairs from tipping backward if we collide.

CRUNCH

There's a version of this sport called Inclusive Zone Basketball, where wheelchair players and running players use different parts of the court. It's one of the few sports where disabled and non-disabled players take part together. But in elite competitions, all players must have a qualifying disability.
The wheels are slanted, which allows me to move and spin in any direction.
WHOOSH
Our wheels are ultra-reinforced to take all the impact.
CRASH
SQUEAK
A bumper on the front stops my feet from getting hurt in the game.
Every part of each player's wheelchair is completely adjustable. I need to make *my* chair just right for *my* body and *my* disability.

28 There's a dark side...

to every table tennis bat.

Professional table tennis bats have two different sides, which are usually red and black. The rubber surface on each side often has a different texture — the ball bounces faster off the red side, and spins off the black side.

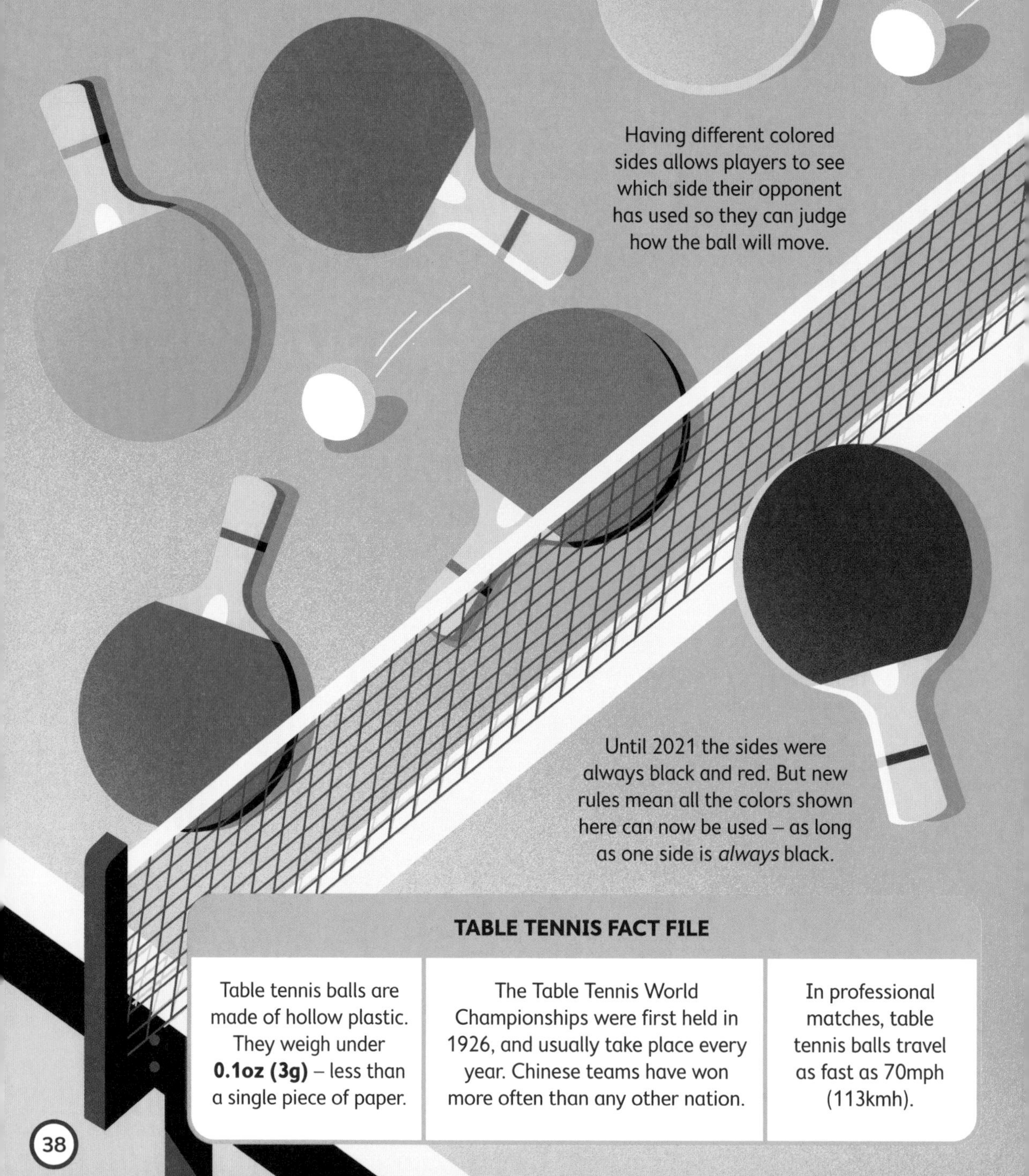

Having different colored sides allows players to see which side their opponent has used so they can judge how the ball will move.

Until 2021 the sides were always black and red. But new rules mean all the colors shown here can now be used — as long as one side is *always* black.

TABLE TENNIS FACT FILE

Table tennis balls are made of hollow plastic. They weigh under **0.1oz (3g)** – less than a single piece of paper.

The Table Tennis World Championships were first held in 1926, and usually take place every year. Chinese teams have won more often than any other nation.

In professional matches, table tennis balls travel as fast as 70mph (113kmh).

29 The Refugee Team...

welcomes athletes who have fled their homes.

In international competitions, athletes usually represent the country they were born in, or where they live. But not everyone is able to do that. Some athletes have to flee their countries and become **refugees** – so how do they compete?

The first ever time a Refugee Team competed was at the Rio de Janeiro Olympics in 2016.

Our team was made up of athletes who had fled their countries to escape war, poor treatment or unfair governments.

In every Olympics now, we compete under the Olympic flag.

The Refugee Team shows that there is a place for everyone in international sports. It will now always have a place in the Olympics.

One member of the 2016 Refugee Team was 18-year-old Yusra Mardini. In 2015 she fled war-torn Syria, swimming for hours and pushing a boat that carried her family.

She settled in Berlin, where she resumed her training. A year later, she swam in the Olympics.

30 There are twenty-five ways...

to win the Tour de France.

The men's Tour de France is a colossal bike race, taking three weeks and covering 2,200 miles (3,500km), mostly through France. There are 25 different ways a cyclist could come out of it as a winner.

The race is split into 21 stages, each lasting a day, and covering around 100 miles (160km). The first person over the finish line each day wins that stage.

21 Stage winners

Young rider

There's a prize for the highest-ranking young rider – under 26 years old.

Points classification

As the riders race, they collect points in mini-sprints along the way. The person with the most sprint points wins the points classification.

King of the Mountains

Riders get points if they're the first up a mountain. The rider with the most mountain points wins the title King of the Mountains.

FINISH

Overall winner

The race usually finishes in Paris. The rider who completes the Tour with the quickest overall time wins.

Usually, the overall winner will have won several stages too. But in theory it's possible for 25 individual riders all to come out as winners.

22

23

24

25

16

17

18

19

20

21

31 Having a mustache...

could make swimmers lose by a hair.

When only a fraction of a second separates winners from losers, hair on a swimmer's body can become a real drag. Each little hair causes resistance as swimmers glide through water, slowing them down.

Swimmers go to great lengths to shave as much time off their race as possible — by shaving off their body hair and wearing a cap on their heads.

This helps them become more streamlined so they can glide faster through water.

32 A retired tennis ball...

makes a perfect mouse house.

Every year, the Wimbledon tennis championship in London uses over 50,000 balls. When it's all over, some of those balls find a new life out in the countryside.

After Wimbledon, some old balls are sold to raise money for charity, and others are sent off to nature reserves and parks around the UK.

With a small entry hole cut into them, tennis balls make ideal homes for wild harvest mice.

These homes protect us from bad weather, and stop predators reaching us, too.

33 You could stay in bed...

and still get better at soccer.

Training, drills and exercise are essential for improving as an athlete. But, by using a technique called **visualization**, you can also sharpen your skills without touching a ball – and without even leaving your bed.

Visualization is a way of training *in your mind*. Over and over again, you focus on what it would look and feel like to perform a skill perfectly. For example, you might imagine...

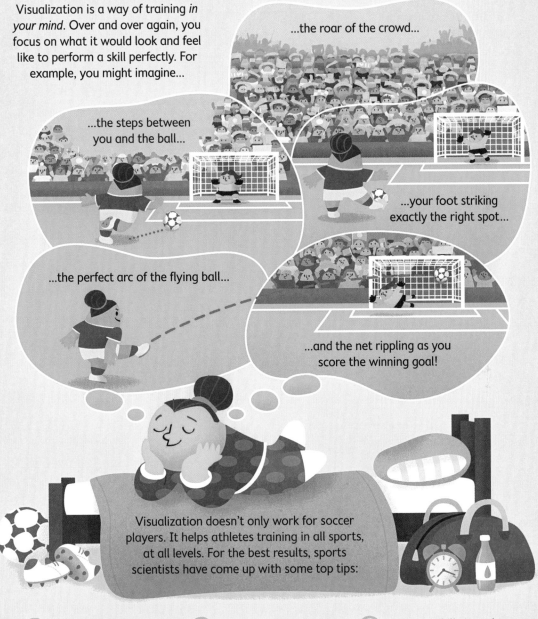

...the roar of the crowd...

...the steps between you and the ball...

...your foot striking exactly the right spot...

...the perfect arc of the flying ball...

...and the net rippling as you score the winning goal!

Visualization doesn't only work for soccer players. It helps athletes training in all sports, at all levels. For the best results, sports scientists have come up with some top tips:

1. Do it regularly and repeatedly – like any kind of training.

2. Spend at least five minutes on each visualization session.

3. Imagine skills in real time to rehearse rhythm and timing.

34 To grow your own cricket bat...

you'll need seeds and patience.

Some pieces of sports equipment are engineered by machines in high-tech factories, with super-modern materials. But some are made from materials you could grow yourself – as long as you're willing to wait...

PLANT THESE SEEDS TO GROW YOUR OWN SPORTS EQUIPMENT

Simply plant in soil.
Drench in water and sunshine.
Wait 10-50 years.
Harvest the mature wood.
Create your sports equipment.
Plant some more!

THE SPORTY SEEDS CO.

Hard maple
Acer saccharum

Qualities of its wood:
Rock-solid wood that can take a lot of impact without breaking.

**Makes:
Bowling pins and skateboards**

TAKES: **25** years

THE SPORTY SEEDS CO.

Koa tree
Acacia koa

Qualities of its wood:
Buoyant wood that doesn't absorb water or swell when wet.

**Makes:
Surfboards**

TAKES: **30** years

While the items listed here have traditionally been made from wood, some are now made from newer materials including carbon fiber and fiberglass.

But cricket bats are always, and *only*, made from white willow wood.

THE SPORTY SEEDS CO.

Ash tree
Fraxinus species

Qualities of its wood:

Hard but slightly flexible wood that provides huge power for hitting.

**Makes:
Baseball bats and hurling sticks**

TAKES: **25** years

THE SPORTY SEEDS CO.

White willow tree
Salix alba

Qualities of its wood:

Tough wood that absorbs shock.

**Makes:
Cricket bats**

TAKES: **20** years

Cricket balls are made from trees, too. They have a core made from cork, the bark of a type of oak tree, surrounded by string.

A leather covering is stitched together over the outside, forming a seam.

Seam •••••→

35 Not all battles...

are fought in armor.

In the 1970s, the world of sports was unequal. Men won more money, more TV time and more opportunities. But, one night in 1973, the face of women's sport changed forever, with a world-famous battle...

The event, known as the **Battle of the Sexes**, was a televised tennis match between women's number 1, Billie Jean King, and retired men's player Bobby Riggs.

Riggs said women couldn't play. He said that they were so much worse that he could beat any woman in the world, even at 55 years old.

Bobby ·········▶
Riggs

◀··········· Billie
Jean King

King won. Her victory was watched by **90 million** people around the world. She proved that female players were just as talented and worthy as their male counterparts.

TENNIS FACT FILE

Even after King's amazing victory, tennis stayed unequal for a while.

It wasn't until 2007 that the men and women were awarded equal prize money at the Wimbledon Championships.

Over £2 million for each singles champion

Men's Wimbledon trophy	Women's Wimbledon plate
There's a pineapple on the top of the trophy, but no one is very sure why.	The plate is covered in etchings of Greek mythology.

The Battle of the Sexes is one of the most watched sporting events ever. No tennis match has ever had so many TV viewers.

Today, tennis still has a lot of viewers. Each year around **400 million people** across the world tune in to the big Grand Slam tournaments.

Major tennis tournaments, known as the Grand Slam

Australian Open – played in Melbourne, Australia in January

French Open – played in Paris, France in May/June

Wimbledon – played in London, UK in June/July

US Open – played in New York, USA in August/September

New balls, please!

In 1972, just before the Battle of the Sexes, tennis balls got switched from white to the yellow we know today.

Tennis was being watched on TV more and more, and white balls weren't picked up very well by the cameras. Bright yellow made them much easier for viewers at home to see.

36 Frozen patterns...

gave figure skating its name.

Modern competitive figure skaters are judged on their leaps and twirls in routines set to music. But before 1990, they were scored on their control and balance, and the intricate patterns they engraved onto the ice.

Skaters had to complete a series of compulsory shapes, including a simple figure of eight.

The most precise shapes, or figures, scored the highest points. But skaters could also create elaborate patterns of their own invention.

Although modern skating competitions no longer judge athletes on their ice figures, skaters today continue to use many of the same movements in their routines.

37 The same stew every day...

is key to sumo success.

Japanese sumo wrestlers, known as **rikishi**, follow a host of strict rules in their everyday lives. The heaviest wrestlers have the biggest advantage in the ring, so these rules even cover mealtimes and how they prepare their food.

We eat the same stew at every meal. It's called *chanko-nabe*, and it's filled with ingredients that provide lots of energy.

From shopping for ingredients to chopping vegetables, we all help to prepare the stew.

Lots of retired sumo wrestlers become chefs, making the stew for hungry customers.

We skip breakfast to work up a bigger appetite. Then, at lunch, we consume ten or more bowls of stew — followed by a rest.

Only six of us can sit around the stew at a time — and the heaviest wrestlers get the first serving.

38 The point of pole vaulting...

hasn't always been to jump the highest.

Pole vaulters at modern track and field events use long, flexible, fiberglass poles to launch themselves over a high bar. But long before competitions such as these were invented, vaulting poles had all kinds of handy uses.

Soldiers in Ancient Egypt used poles to leap over the walls of enemy cities they were invading.

Ancient Greeks held pole vaulting competitions, but before that they used poles to mount their horses.

Around 500 years ago, messengers delivered news across England. They relied on their poles to leap over obstacles, using one end to carry bread for the journey.

For centuries, people in the Netherlands kept stacks of poles outside their houses to help them hop over canals.

Today, professional athletes use flexible, high-tech poles to jump roughly three times their body height.

39 It takes an Acme Thunderer...

to cut through the din.

Whistles are an essential tool used by thousands of referees every week. But they were invented in 1880 initially as a tool for the police, making a noise so loud they could be heard a mile away.

Before the 1880s, soccer referees signaled to players by waving a handkerchief.

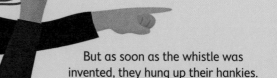

But as soon as the whistle was invented, they hung up their hankies.

40 The fastest race cars...

could drive upside down.

Race cars whizz around tracks at such high speeds that they risk skidding off. So, engineers design cars to have as much grip as possible. In fact, they make them *so* grippy that they *could* drive upside down.

As the car reaches high speeds, air rushes over carefully designed wings and bodywork. This pushes the car into the track with enormous force.

This force is several times greater than the weight of the car itself. It increases grip, allowing the car to race around corners faster.

Acme is still the world's largest producer of whistles, making over five million a year – most of which are used for refereeing sports.

Meanwhile, refs in deaf soccer matches still use handkerchiefs.

In theory, at great speed, the car generates enough force that it could drive on an upside-down track.

Unfortunately, even if there were upside-down race tracks, we wouldn't be seeing races on them anytime soon. That's because the engine wouldn't work upside down.

Not to mention the motion sickness drivers would face...

41 Words as sharp as arrows...

win the game of Da.

In the kingdom of Bhutan, the game of **Da** – or archery – is the national sport, played in every village. It is a key part of culture and society. And it involves far more than just shooting arrows at a target...

Matches are major events. Teams of archers shoot at targets over several days, trying to build up enough points to win.

But in addition to shooting, archers compete in a battle of words. Teams hurl poetic insults at the opposition, and throngs of onlookers chant along as well.

Your arrow is so aimless it will never hit the mark!

You hold that bow and arrow like you're shooting in the dark!

Your arrow looks like kindling that is begging for a spark!

These insults are designed to intimidate archers and mess up their shot. They have been a part of the sport for thousands of years.

Football's the name...

but *kicking* the ball is just one part of the game.

Many sports have the word "football" somewhere in their name, but players don't have to rely solely on their feet. In fact, in most types of football, players can use various parts of their bodies to score points.

Circles indicate parts of the body used to score in each type of football.

American football

Players score points by holding the ball in the opposition's end of the field, known as the end zone, or by kicking the ball between a pair of posts.

Association football

Usually referred to as football or soccer. Players score by kicking the ball into a goal, *or* they can use their chests, knees or heads. However, research linking heading with brain injuries has led to bans in some places.

Gaelic football

Players score by kicking the ball, *or* hitting it with their hand, into a goal, or between two posts.

Australian rules football

Players can pass to each other by kicking the ball, or hitting it with their hands. But to score points, players *must* kick the ball between posts.

Rugby football

In rugby football, there are just two ways to score: players can either kick the ball between two posts, *or* place it on the ground at the opposition's end of the pitch, known as the in-goal area.

43 Fans who come to cheer...

could stay to play.

Ice hockey is a rough and physical game, so players often get injured. That's why, in an emergency, teams from the National Hockey League (NHL) in the US and Canada may turn to their fans for help on the ice.

Players face many dangers during NHL games.

Strong, springy hockey sticks

Skates with sharp steel blades

A hard rubber puck flying at 100 miles (160km) per hour

Players are allowed to crash into one another at full speed, bashing opponents into the boards surrounding the ice. This is known as **checking**.

Tempers flare, and fights often break out on the ice.

AN ICE HOCKEY HOLIDAY

For decades, international ice hockey has been dominated by a group of nations known as the Big Six: Canada, the US, Russia, the Czech Republic, Finland, and Sweden.

It is rare for other nations to succeed in major competitions. *So* rare, that when Latvia won the *bronze medal* at the 2023 world championships, the country declared a national holiday.

Despite wearing heavy padding, gloves and helmets, players *do* get injured.

There are back-up players called **reserves**, waiting to go on the ice if anyone's injuries are bad enough that they can't continue playing.

But if the goalie *and* reserve goalie become injured, a team may call on anyone available — including spectators — to join the game and defend the goal.

This happened during an NHL game in 2020. The Carolina Hurricanes signed an emergency, one-game contract with a spectator — a retired player from the lower leagues.

He borrowed some equipment, jumped onto the ice, and helped his team to victory.

Go get them, Dad!

Going for a run...

could expose military secrets.

Information about a country's military is highly sensitive. Many military bases and outposts don't appear on maps at all, and their locations are closely guarded secrets – secrets that were once revealed by runners.

Lots of people have sports apps on their watches, phones or other wearable devices. These can record their runs, hikes and bike rides.

One day in 2017, a popular app released detailed maps showing the activities of *all* its users around the world.

The maps showed over **2 million routes** that people had logged using their devices.

Thicker, brighter lines showed where lots of people's routes overlapped.

Cities in the maps glowed bright, full of routes.

Remote areas
and wilderness
remained dark.

But, unexpectedly, out in
the darkness, gleaming trails
showed activity in places far
from known towns.

It turned out these were
routes recorded by soldiers
running or walking. And
they revealed the locations
of top-secret bases.

This potential security threat was quickly spotted and corrected
– and since then, app designers and governments have worked
closely to ensure that it doesn't happen again.

45 Taking the train...

keeps sumo wrestlers safe.

Sumo wrestlers, or **rikishi**, are not allowed to drive, to avoid accidents. This means in Japan, they can often be seen on buses and trains.

The rules about wrestlers' clothes and appearance make them easy to spot.

46 Be as fast as a mantis...

to master tángláng quán.

Tángláng quán is one of an incredible variety of self-defence sports known as **martial arts**. Some involve rapid, insect-like strikes; others focus on slow, flowing movements. Here are just a few examples.

Martial arts are extraordinarily popular.

It's estimated that **100 million** people around the world do **karate**, a Japanese martial art.

An estimated **70 million** people do the Korean martial art **taekwondo**. It's been an Olympic sport since 2000.

Tángláng quán

Origin: China

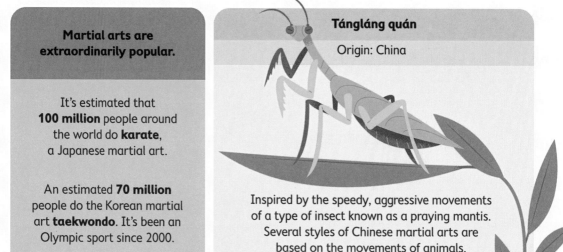

Inspired by the speedy, aggressive movements of a type of insect known as a praying mantis. Several styles of Chinese martial arts are based on the movements of animals.

They must wear their hair in a topknot style, known as **chonmage**, when they're out and about.

Whenever they're in public, rikishi must wear traditional robes called **yukata**.

Junior rikishi have to wear wooden sandals known as **geta**. Senior wrestlers, like the one to the left, wear straw sandals called **zori**.

Sumo

Origin: Japan

An ancient form of wrestling. Wrestlers use powerful pulling and pushing moves to force their opponent outside a fighting ring, or to the ground.

Nguni stick-fighting

Origin: South Africa

Fighters are armed with two sticks. One is used to carry out fast attacking strikes. The other is used for defensive blocks.

Tai chi

Origin: China

Involves performing set sequences of slow movements with a focus on defense and physical fitness.

There are LOADS more martial arts, such as:

Mongolian wrestling	
Capoeira	Aikido
Jujutsu	Judo
Greco-Roman wrestling	
Coreeda	Boxing
Fencing	Muay Thai

47 Competing in the nude...

was the norm in Ancient Greece.

Modern athletes take their sportswear very seriously. A baggy top or worn-out shoe could be the difference between victory and defeat. Ancient Greek athletes had no such worries – they competed naked.

Historians have several theories about why Ancient Greek athletes competed with nothing on. It might have been...

...a safety measure, after someone tripped and fell on an unraveled loincloth.

...a tribute to Zeus, King of the Gods, to show him how strong and athletic they were.

...a way to intimidate other competitors.

Whatever the reason, Ancient Greek nudity is behind some of the terms we use to talk about sports today. The Greek word for naked was *gymnos*, which is where the words "gymnasium" and "gymnastics" come from.

48 Sandpaper, spit and sweat...

turn balls into rule-breakers.

Rule-breaking might conjure up images of athletes taking performance-enhancing drugs or fouling their opponents. But some rules are broken in less obvious ways, by making barely noticeable changes to a ball.

Footballs are easier to throw and catch when they're soft. So, rule-breaking teams might let a little air out of them.

Some tennis players have been caught scuffing balls to make them fluffy and slow, or rubbing them with sweat to make them smoother and faster.

TENNIS BALL

Cricket players have been known to rough-up one side of the ball with sandpaper or dirt. This causes the ball to fly sideways as it's bowled, making it harder to hit.

Rogue pitchers might apply spit or oils to one side of the baseball. This adds a small, but significant, amount of weight — and the ball moves unpredictably as it slips out of the pitcher's hand.

FOOTBALL

CRICKET BALL

BASEBALL

49 A ship setting sail...

put an end to the longest cricket match.

In a type of cricket match called a **test match**, two international teams compete over several days. These games are now limited to a maximum of five days – but until 1939, some matches had no time limit.

DAY ONE

On March 3rd, 1939, England and South Africa started playing a test match in Durban, South Africa. In a test match, both teams take two turns batting.

South Africa batted first...

DAY TWO

...and kept batting.

DAY THREE

Today's a rest day!

Z Z Z

DAY FOUR

South Africa were *still* batting.

Late in the day, it was finally England's turn to bat.

DAY FIVE

Ticket prices were cut in an attempt to attract fans to an increasingly dull match.

Get your half-price tickets here!

DAY SIX

England missed a ship to Cape Town, which would have eventually taken them home...

...because they were only just finishing their first turn batting, before South Africa started batting again.

MATCH LENGTHS

Today, international cricket matches come in three lengths.

Match type	Twenty20	One Day International	Test
Max. length	Three hours	Nine hours	Five days
Each team bats	Once	Once	Twice
Max. balls bowled	240	600	Roughly 2,700

DAY SEVEN

South Africa continued batting.

Yawn...

DAY EIGHT

England started their second turn batting.

Here we go again!

DAY NINE

Play was paused while they waited for the rain to clear.

DAY TEN

The rain's stopped – we can play!

Umm, no we can't! Today's a rest day.

DAY ELEVEN

England resumed batting.

We only need 200 runs to win!

DAY TWELVE

Just 42 runs to win, but if we don't leave *now*, we'll miss our ship!

Twelve grueling days after it started, the match was called off – *without* a winner.

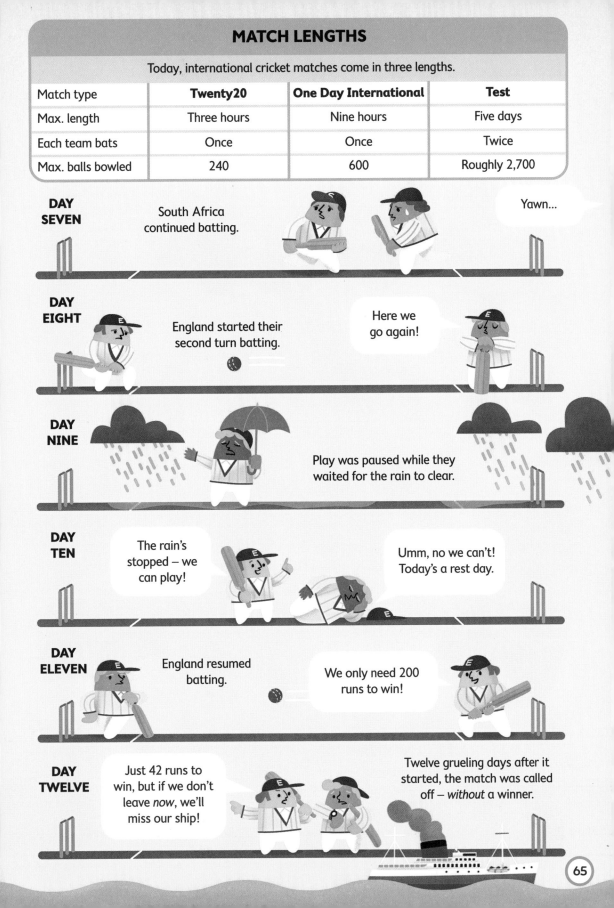

50 A sporting clash...

led to a change of identity.

Sports are an important part of a nation's identity, uniting people in support of their country's teams around the world. But one Olympic Games led two countries to change their identities – or at least, their flags.

In 1936, athletes from around the world arrived in Germany to compete in the Berlin Olympics.

Each team was identified by its national flag. But there was a problem no one had spotted before.

The flags of Haiti and Liechtenstein were practically identical.

Haiti, in the Caribbean, is 5,000 miles (8,000km) away from Liechtenstein, in Europe.

At that time, international travel and communications were far more limited than they are today. It was the first time the two countries had competed against each other.

HAITI

LIECHTENSTEIN

The following year, both countries changed their flags by adding emblems to them.

Haiti added a palm tree...

...while Liechtenstein opted for a royal crown.

Now we can be told apart.

No more mix-ups!

HAITI

LIECHTENSTEIN

51 A marathon runner in space...

went around the world twice.

In 2007, Sunita Williams made history by competing in a marathon from her treadmill on the International Space Station. In the course of her marathon, she ran all the way around the world – twice.

The low gravity in a space station means astronauts' muscles aren't working hard. So to stay strong and healthy, astronauts have to run for several hours a day, strapped to specialized treadmills.

Sunita Williams took this one step further, and ran a whole marathon – 26 miles (42km.)

She had an official race number.

For snacks, she ate pieces of oranges.

Water was provided in a pouch with a straw.

She completed it in 4 hours, 24 minutes.

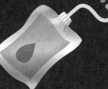

04:24

While she was running, the space station was moving at 17,130 miles (27,580km) per hour. It zoomed all the way around the world more than twice and saw two sunrises.

52 Singing spectators...

could help you win.

A team playing in its own stadium can count on plenty of supporters there to cheer, chant and applaud. But this noise doesn't just make for an exciting game – sports psychologists have found that it seems to give the home team a huge advantage.

Scientists have observed that teams playing in their own stadiums tend to win more games than they lose. They call this **home advantage**.

Can you hear us...

...stamp and ROAR?

Home teams are familiar with their own equipment and less disrupted by travel. They also usually have more fans spectating than the opposing team.

Sports psychologists think that an encouraging crowd can boost the home team's morale, and even make the players feel less tired.

The more we cheer...

...the more you score!

So next time you have a competition, invite your friends along to cheer you on. It might just help you win.

53 Stadiums of the future...

could be here today, gone tomorrow.

Most stadiums are huge constructions of steel and concrete, blazing with energy-hungry lights. People drive or fly long distances to get to them. But what if there was a way that was better for the environment? Architects have come up with the following ideas.

Multi-purpose

A stadium built of individual sections, or modules, can be taken apart and re-used as something else. This happened to a stadium built of sea containers after the Qatar World Cup in 2022.

Covered in plants

Covering a stadium's walls or roof in plants would make the air cleaner by absorbing lots of harmful carbon dioxide.

Local

With holographic technology, you could visit a local stadium to watch a 3D hologram of a game beamed in from the other side of the world. That means less flying and less fuel used.

54 Six minutes a day...

is all the time a skeleton champion spends on ice.

In skeleton, athletes plummet face-first on a sled down a narrow, icy track at incredibly high speeds. The sport is so physically exhausting that athletes can only train on the ice for about six minutes a day.

> When I'm on the ice, I'm on a thin sled called a skeleton, like this! But I can only train on the ice in short bursts.

This shows how a normal day of training for a skeleton athlete might be broken down.

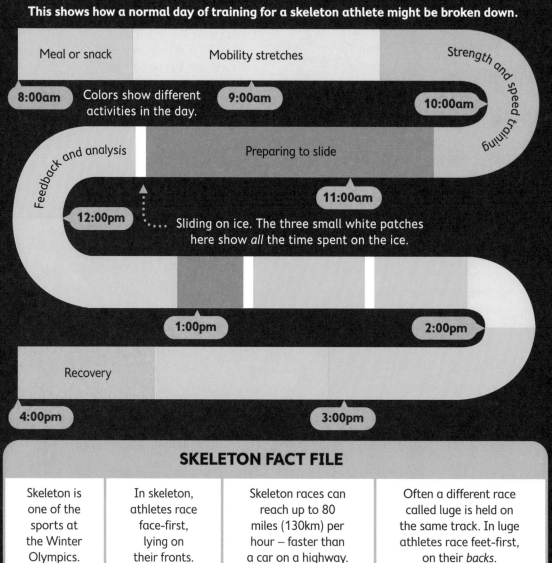

Meal or snack

Mobility stretches

Strength and speed training

8:00am

Colors show different activities in the day.

9:00am

10:00am

Feedback and analysis

Preparing to slide

11:00am

12:00pm

Sliding on ice. The three small white patches here show *all* the time spent on the ice.

1:00pm

2:00pm

Recovery

4:00pm

3:00pm

SKELETON FACT FILE

Skeleton is one of the sports at the Winter Olympics.	In skeleton, athletes race face-first, lying on their fronts.	Skeleton races can reach up to 80 miles (130km) per hour – faster than a car on a highway.	Often a different race called luge is held on the same track. In luge athletes race feet-first, on their *backs*.

55 Understanding physics...

helped an athlete jump higher.

For hundreds of years, high jumpers tried a range of different methods to leap cleanly over a bar. Then, in 1968, an engineering student and athlete named Dick Fosbury used his knowledge of physics and decided to jump backwards. It changed high jump forever.

To jump high, you need to beat the force of gravity, which is always pulling you down.

FRONT-FIRST TECHNIQUES

WESTERN ROLL

STRADDLE

SCISSOR KICK

Fosbury figured out that the best and most efficient way to jump was to go *back-first* over the bar.

The physics of his method meant he could jump *higher*, with *less* effort.

TIMES TODAY
FOSBURY FLOPS!

Fosbury first did this in an international competition at the 1968 Olympic Games in Mexico City, and won. This technique is now called the **Fosbury flop**, and today it's what *every* competitive high jumper does.

56 We might not be the fastest...

but we can run the furthest.

Sports competitions celebrate the strongest, fastest and toughest people in the world. But compared to other animals, our best *isn't* always exceptional...

FASTEST SWIMMER

Human
Around **5.5mph (9km/h)**

Marlin
Over **22mph (35km/h)**

FASTEST MARATHON RUNNER

26 miles (42km)

Human
Around
2 hours

Ostrich 45 mins
The tendons in ostriches' legs are really springy, which prevents them from getting tired.

LONGEST RUNNER

Wolf
Over **30 miles (50km)**
a day at a slow trot.

This is *one* thing that humans are actually the best at.

LONGEST JUMPER

Human
Around **30ft (9m)**

Kangaroo
Around **46ft (14m)**

FASTEST SPRINTER

Human
Top speeds of **27mph (44km/h)**

Cheetah
Top speeds of **62mph (100km/h)**

BEST SOCCER PLAYER

Humans probably take the crown here, too. But they're not the *only* animals that can play soccer.

In one study, scientists taught bees to use their legs to score goals with a tiny ball, in return for a sugary treat. It worked – and the bees could play their own little game.

HIGHEST JUMPER

Compared to their size, **fleas** can jump highest – over **100** times the length of their bodies.

Dolphin
26ft (8m)
right out of the water

Human
Around
8ft (2.5m)

Humans cool down by sweating – something furry animals can't do. That makes us more efficient and enables us to keep running for longer.

Human
Over **100 miles (160km)**

Compared to their size, **fleas** can jump furthest – around **200** times the length of their bodies.

57 Some sailboats don't sail...
they fly.

The oldest international competition in any sport is a sailing race called the **America's Cup**. It has been going since 1851 and is mostly unchanged – except for the boats, which are new and very high-tech. *So* high-tech, in fact, that they can fly.

This is one of several types of boats used in today's sailing competitions. It is a **catamaran**, meaning it is constructed from two **hulls** joined together side by side.

Main sail The sail is solid, and built in sections.

Hulls Made of super-light, super-strong carbon fiber

These hulls have a large surface area, and wherever they touch the water, they create drag, slowing the boat down.

So, the boat is designed to ride on high-tech blades called **hydrofoils**. As the vessel picks up speed, these blades lift it completely *out* of the water — reducing drag and enabling it to travel at *four times* the speed of the wind — up to **62 miles (100km)** per hour.

Hydrofoil

How do hydrofoils work?

Water rushing over the curved surface of a foil creates lift. This is the same effect as air rushing over the wing of a plane.

58 A boat that flies...

draws rival spies.

In some races, competitors must all use the same type of boat, but they *can* modify the shape and size of the foils. That – along with the crew's sailing skills – is what sets the winners apart. So it's common for rival teams to spy on one another.

Boat builders spend months modifying and refining their designs in heavily guarded boat sheds. But when it's time to test the new foils at sea, the spies come out.

If we know how *their* team's designers changed their blades, *our* team can try to do even better!

Pass me the binoculars! I need to see their blades.

Ohhh! They're really flying. Have they made the foils longer? Shorter? Thicker?

SAILING FACT FILE

In the **America's Cup**, just two boats race each other. The competition takes its name from the first ever winner, a yacht called *America*.

In **Olympic sailing** competitions, many boats race to finish a course first. They race over 10 times, and get 1 point for coming first, 2 for second and so on. The team with the **fewest** points at the end wins.

Olympic windsurfing competitions use the same hydrofoil technology. The hydrofoil lifts a board, rather than a boat, out of the water.

59 Athletes have to pee...

whenever they're asked to.

There are some drugs that can enhance an athlete's performance – so they're banned to keep competitions fair. To check that athletes haven't taken any banned substances, officials can visit them at *any time*. The athlete must provide a blood or urine sample *whenever* they are asked.

60 Shuttlecocks fly faster...

on Mount Fuji.

In badminton, shuttlecocks whoosh through the air at up to 250 miles (400km) per hour, making it the fastest racket sport. But in *some* places, shuttlecocks fly *faster* and *further* than others.

Air is made up of tiny molecules. But the higher up you go, the more spread-out these molecules become, and the easier it is for shuttlecocks to whoosh through the air.

This means a shuttlecock would fly faster and further up here on Mount Fuji in Japan –

12,390ft (3,776m)
above sea level...

...than it would if you hit it with the same force down here on Bondi Beach in Australia, just

69ft (21m)
above sea level.

Although the same principle also applies to sports that use balls, the shuttlecock's light weight makes the effects of altitude more noticeable.

So engineers have created a range of shuttlecocks. Lightweight shuttlecocks twirl easily through the thick air of low altitudes, while heavier ones suit thin air higher up.

61 A wrestling princess...

broke hearts and won horses.

In Mongolian wrestling, or **bokh**, wrestlers have one goal: to make their opponent touch the ground with any body part that isn't their feet. Bokh is very popular in Mongolia today, just as it was 800 years ago in the time of one of the greatest wrestlers of all: a princess named Khutulun.

Khutulun refused to marry any man who couldn't beat her in a wrestling match. If they lost, they had to hand over their horses to her.

Such was Khutulun's skill, she is said to have won over ten thousand horses by defeating would-be husbands.

FOLK WRESTLING

Unlike some forms of wrestling which take place at international competitions, bokh is one of many traditional styles, known as folk wrestling, that belong to particular regions...

Tigel	Kene	Huka-huka
Traditional Ethiopian wrestling. Wrestlers' right shoulders must be in contact at all times.	Form of wrestling practiced by the Naga people of northeastern India and Myanmar.	Style of the Xingu people of Brazil. Matches take place at a festival to celebrate the dead.

62 Bronze beats silver...

when happiness is the prize.

When it comes to medals, the winner gets gold, second gets silver and third gets bronze. So, it sounds as though bronze is a worse prize than silver – but studies have shown that athletes who come third are often happier with their result.

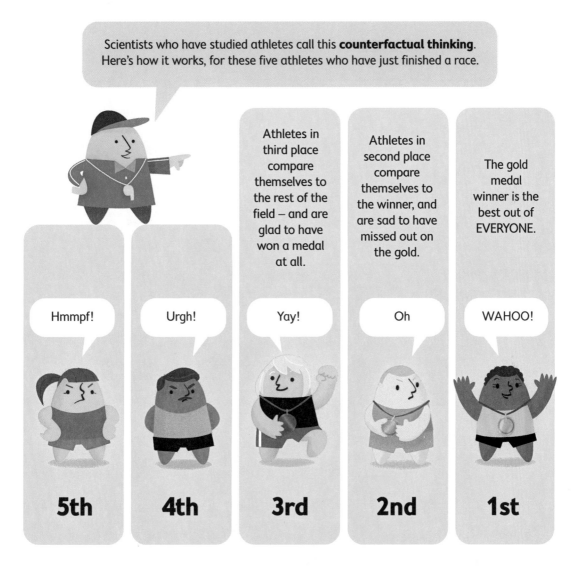

Scientists who have studied athletes call this **counterfactual thinking**. Here's how it works, for these five athletes who have just finished a race.

Athletes in third place compare themselves to the rest of the field – and are glad to have won a medal at all.

Athletes in second place compare themselves to the winner, and are sad to have missed out on the gold.

The gold medal winner is the best out of EVERYONE.

Hmmpf!

Urgh!

Yay!

Oh

WAHOO!

5th

4th

3rd

2nd

1st

This effect, sometimes called **silver medal syndrome**, is particularly strong if the top three finish close together.

63 Grass is grass...

but not just *any* grass will do.

It may *look* ordinary – but the green stuff beneath an athlete's feet is never just *any* grass. At many sports grounds, experts select species and types of grass to suit the climate, soil and sport being played.

HOW TO PICK THE BEST GRASS VARIETIES:

IN A COOL CLIMATE

Rye grass is widely used in cool climates for cricket, rugby, tennis and hockey. It's a tough, dark green variety that can withstand heavy use.

IN TROPICAL PLACES

In extreme heat, rye grass may wilt or wither underfoot. But **Bermuda grass** remains lush and green: a winning choice for the sunniest cricket grounds.

FOR A SMOOTH SURFACE

This mix of **bentgrass** and **slender creeping red fescue** is ideal for lawn bowls. It can be cut *extra* short, which keeps balls rolling smoothly.

ARTIFICIAL TURF

This is suited to places where it's too cold or dry for grass to grow. It *looks* like lush, natural turf, but this surface is made from thick, durable **plastic**.

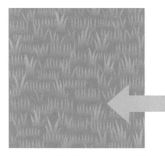

A HARDWEARING HYBRID

On some professional football pitches, real grass is combined with millions of blades of **artificial grass**. These are sewn into the ground by large machines.

HYBRID TURF FACTS:

Stays green in all weathers.

Provides a more even playing surface than natural grass and needs less maintenance.

Artificial tufts reinforce and protect the roots of the natural grass.

Lasts up to four times longer than a regular grass field.

64 Ice is ice...

but not just *any* ice will do.

Many winter sports take place on ice. While all ice rinks are made from frozen water, not all icy surfaces are the same. Each sport requires ice of a particular temperature, hardness and texture.

THE BEST SURFACES FOR ICE SPORTS:

A SOFTER SURFACE

Figure skating requires softer ice than most ice sports. The rink is kept at about **27°F (-3°C)**, so it's not too hard for big jumps and landings.

DIAMOND HARD

Speed skating requires super-cold, super-hard ice. It is kept at about **19°F (-7°C)** so that skaters race *over* its frozen surface, without cutting *into* it and slowing down.

SUPER FOR SLIDING

For curling competitions, **tiny droplets** are frozen on top of the ice rink between each round of play. These icy bumps help curling stones slide extra-far.

ARTIFICIAL ICE

The first indoor ice rinks were built in 1841. Freezing a room full of water wasn't possible then, so the "ice" was made mostly from **lard** – which was slippery, but a bit smelly.

PAINTED LINES

Ice hockey is played on rinks with clearly marked lines. To make these lines, bold **red, white and blue paints** are added between several layers of frozen water.

ICE RINK FACTS:

Ice rinks are maintained using big sit-on machines that sweep across the rink laying down a clean layer of water, which freezes instantly to create a fresh, smooth surface.

65 There are no limits...

on the size of a kilikiti team.

In the early 1800s, English people introduced cricket to Samoa. The Samoans quickly transformed it into their own game, called **kilikiti**. Today, this ultra-inclusive game is Samoa's national sport.

Unlike cricket, and most other sports, a kilikiti team has no set size. Entire villages compete against one another, and some matches have involved hundreds of people.

You don't need any specialist equipment or protective clothing to play kilikiti — just wear a traditional Polynesian skirt, called a **lavalava**.

Age or gender doesn't matter on the kilikiti field — anyone who turns up can play.

Can I play?

Sure!

Despite efforts to develop standard rules, such as fixed team sizes, traditional kilikiti games remain popular in Samoa.

66 Fill a top hat with feathers...

to make the first proper golf ball.

Until the 17th century, golf was played with wooden balls that were probably used for lots of other games, too. That changed when the first specially-designed golf ball was created. It was called a **featherie**.

To make a featherie:

1

Sew a small leather pouch and soak it in water.

2

Find exactly enough feathers to fill a top hat.

3

Boil the feathers, then stuff them into the leather pouch and stitch it shut.

4

As the feathers cool and the leather dries, it will shrink and contract into a small, hard ball.

Featheries were used for 200 years. But the balls were lumpy so they didn't always fly straight.

Modern golf balls consist of a large rubber core covered in a strong outer layer of plastic.

Some balls have extra layers of rubber between the core and cover. These layers help players to add spin to the ball.

67 A tennis champion by day...

was a housekeeper by night.

In the 1920s and '30s, a tennis player named Ora Washington was winning back-to-back matches and national competitions. But after the matches, she would go back to her other job.

At the time, America was racially divided. Washington wasn't allowed to be part of the country's biggest tennis association because she was Black. She had to join a different league instead — but she won match after match.

She wasn't just a tennis champion — she was a basketball champion as well. Some newspapers called her Queen Ora.

But most white Americans hadn't heard of her. Throughout and after her sports career, she continued to work as a housekeeper to support herself.

Washington didn't receive the wide-spread recognition or fame she deserved, but today she is remembered as a sports superstar

68 Eleven minutes...

is the *actual* length of a football game.

When it's broadcast on TV, a typical National Football League (NFL) game lasts around three hours. But only *eleven minutes* of that is spent on actual game play. So what is shown for the rest of the time?

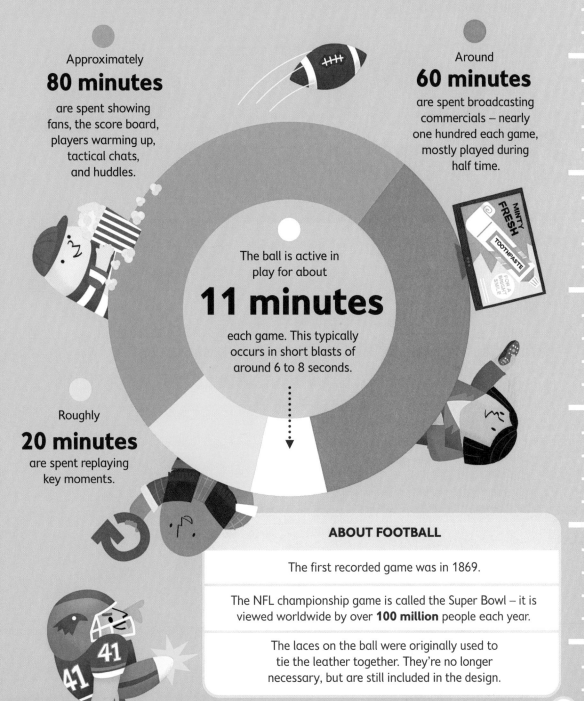

Approximately

80 minutes

are spent showing fans, the score board, players warming up, tactical chats, and huddles.

Around

60 minutes

are spent broadcasting commercials – nearly one hundred each game, mostly played during half time.

The ball is active in play for about

11 minutes

each game. This typically occurs in short blasts of around 6 to 8 seconds.

Roughly

20 minutes

are spent replaying key moments.

MINTY FRESH

TOOTHPASTE

FOR A BRIGHT SMILE

ABOUT FOOTBALL

The first recorded game was in 1869.

The NFL championship game is called the Super Bowl – it is viewed worldwide by over **100 million** people each year.

The laces on the ball were originally used to tie the leather together. They're no longer necessary, but are still included in the design.

69 Romans trained for war...

by doing gymnastics.

Two thousand years ago, Roman soldiers prepared for battle by mounting and dismounting a wooden horse as quickly as they could.

Today, gymnasts perform twists and turns on a modern version of the same equipment, now known as the pommel horse.

70 Pink underpants...

are against the rules for baseball umpires.

Umpires in Major League Baseball (MLB) have to abide by a long and strict set of rules. One of them is the instruction that they must *only* wear black underwear.

It's my job to watch all the balls being pitched at the batter, so I do a lot of bending down and squatting.

So if my pants ever split, no one would notice, because I *should* be wearing black underwear!

A powerful punch...

can fight a flame without touching it.

In a group of Chinese martial arts, known as Nei Jia, athletes are required to train their mental focus as well as physical technique. To do this, they must first learn to harness the power of something called **jin**.

Jin describes an athlete's ability to generate an explosive force aimed at a single point. This requires strong mental focus.

To train jin, martial artists attempt to put out a candle flame, without touching it, using the force of a single punch.

At first, the flame might wobble without going out. But as the athlete's force and focus improve, they can extinguish the flame completely. This is a sign that they are prepared for combat.

in a drawer, in a river or on display.

Medals and trophies are worth more than the metal they're made from. They represent a huge achievement after years of training. But what do athletes do with them when the awards ceremony is over?

Follow the lines to see where some awards have ended up.

Sold for $1,000,000

In 2012, Ukrainian boxer Wladimir Klitschko auctioned off his gold medal to raise money for Ukrainian children. He made a million dollars – and the buyer returned the medal to him.

Made into a wedding ring

In 1924, British sprinter Harold Abrahams became the 100m sprint champion. He later carved a strip off his medal to make a wedding ring for his wife.

Thrown into a river

In 1960, Black American boxer Muhammad Ali, then known as Cassius Clay, won gold. But when he returned home, white people in his racially-divided home town still didn't welcome him. It is said that, in anger, he threw his medal in the Ohio River. Years later, he was given a replacement.

Taken away

If an athlete is found to have taken banned substances to gain an unfair advantage, their medals are taken away. After the 2011 World Championship athletics competition, ten medals were stripped – that's around one for every 14 medals handed out.

Stored in a trophy room

By the time tennis champion Serena Williams retired in 2022, she had won almost 100 major titles, trophies and medals. She has dedicated an entire room to storing them.

Hidden at home

Because medals are so valuable, some athletes have chosen to hide them. One kept them in a sock drawer; another said she put them in a kitchen cupboard – because it was an unlikely place for thieves to look.

73 Nearly every curling stone...

comes from Fairy Rock.

Curling is a winter sport played using a big granite stone. You can find granite all over the world, but almost all competition curling stones come from granite taken from just *one* tiny Scottish island.

AILSA CRAIG
SCOTLAND

Ailsa Craig means *fairy rock* in Gaelic.

So how do you play?

In a game of curling, players push stones toward the target area. They **sweep** the ice with brushes to help the stone glide.

Plastic handle

Granite stone

What makes this granite special?

Granite from Ailsa Crag is ideal, because it absorbs very little water. That makes it really hard to crack. It's also very smooth so glides cleanly across the ice.

74 Hasty scribbles...

guide rally drivers to victory.

Rallying is a motorsport that doesn't take place on a racing circuit. Instead, cars zoom along winding tracks and country roads. There are too many twists and turns for drivers to memorize the route in advance, so they rely on a co-driver for directions.

The pair will usually scout out the route together twice before each race. The co-driver scribbles coded notes, called **pacenotes**, recording each turn and obstacle. They relay those notes to the driver during the race.

Pacenotes	Co-driver's instructions	Driver's translation of instructions
L6 Vlg 100 R4	Left six, very long. one hundred, right four.	OK, so that's a flat out left turn that goes on for a while. Then 100 yards of straight road, followed by a medium right turn.
R1 → L1 200)(	Right one, into left one, two hundred, bridge.	Yikes, a hairpin turn right, immediately followed by a hairpin left. Then we have to cross a bridge in 200 yards.
L3 ! bmp 50 jmp stay L	Left three, caution bump, fifty, jump, stay left.	That's a medium left with a big bump. Then it's 50 yards until a jump. I need to stay on the left of the road to land safely.
R2 d.c. slp	Right two, don't cut, slippy.	Ooh, a tight right turn with an obstacle on the inside. I better not cut the corner. Oh, AND it's slippery!

Corners come thick and fast in rallying, so co-drivers give short, snappy instructions. Drivers have to be able to translate descriptions of upcoming corners while keeping the car under control at high speeds.

75 Medals are heard...

as well as seen.

The medals that were given out at the Rio de Janeiro Paralympic Games in 2016 contained tiny steel balls. When they were shaken, the gold, silver and bronze medals each made a distinct sound. This enabled visually-impaired athletes to tell them apart.

Gold
With 28 steel balls inside each gold medal, these sounded the loudest.

Silver
These contained 20.

Bronze
With 16 steel balls inside each bronze, these sounded the softest.

All Olympic medals are the same size. So, for each Olympic Games, designers come up with a new way for visually impaired athletes to tell one from another.

76 Blind skiers hear...

how to navigate the slopes.

You're hurtling down a steep mountainside at over 62 miles (100km) per hour. The wind is whistling, as trees, bumps and ridges loom towards you. Now imagine that you can't see... You need to rely on your *ears* instead.

NOW *Turn* Up MOVE *Bump!* FLAT *Turn* MOVE *Up* TWIST FLAT Up

A lump! *Turn* MOVE Up

TWIST FLAT Up

MOVE TWIST FLAT Up *Turn*

Bump!

Visually-impaired athletes ski with a **guide**. Both wear a wireless headset.

The guide skis slightly ahead, and talks into their headset, telling the athlete *exactly* what to expect on the slope.

Because they train together day after day, the guide can communicate even tricky moves to the skier with very simple, single-word instructions.

77 Plummeting skydivers... talk with their hands.

Diving out of a plane is an extreme sport that requires careful planning and lots of training. To communicate with each other as they whoosh through the air, skydivers use a series of hand gestures.

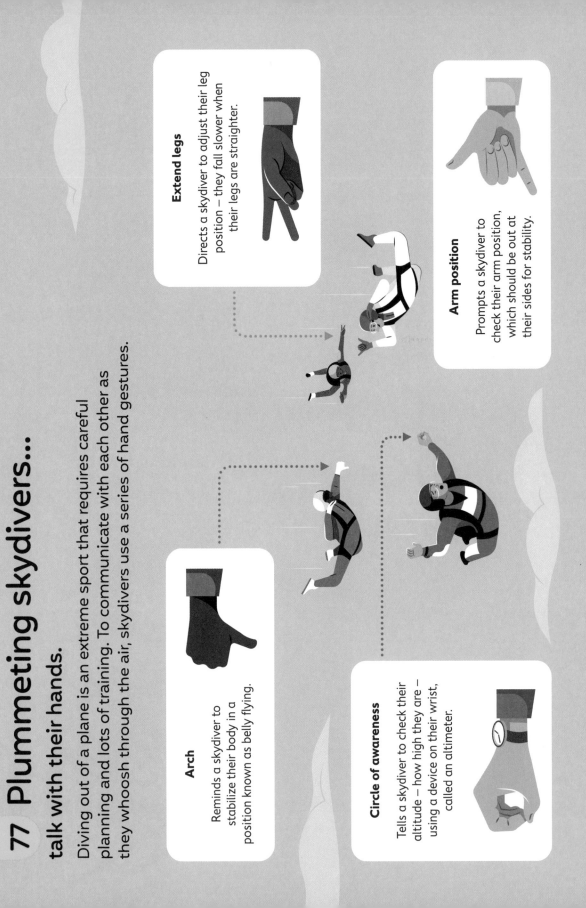

Extend legs

Directs a skydiver to adjust their leg position – they fall slower when their legs are straighter.

Arm position

Prompts a skydiver to check their arm position, which should be out at their sides for stability.

Arch

Reminds a skydiver to stabilize their body in a position known as belly flying.

Circle of awareness

Tells a skydiver to check their altitude – how high they are – using a device on their wrist, called an altimeter.

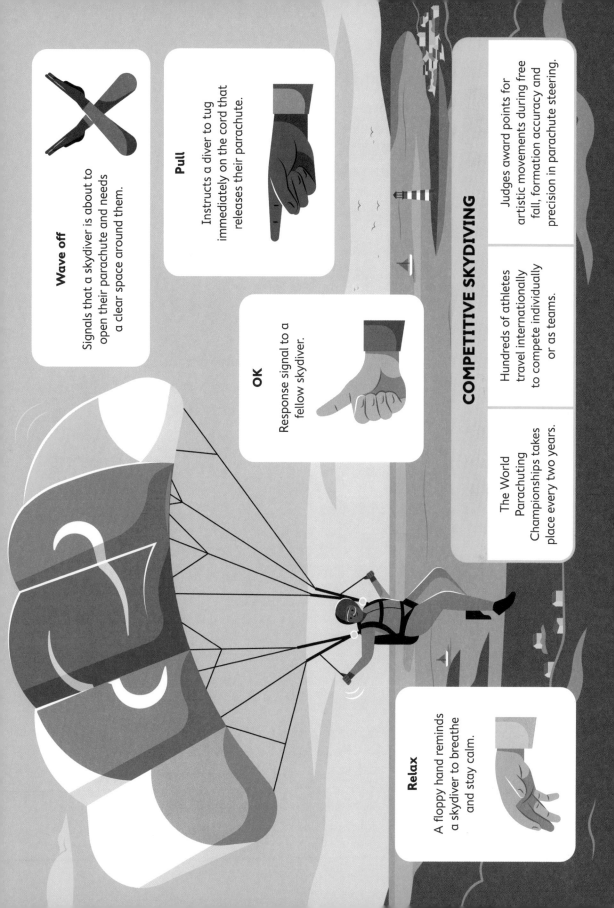

Wave off

Signals that a skydiver is about to open their parachute and needs a clear space around them.

Pull

Instructs a diver to tug immediately on the cord that releases their parachute.

OK

Response signal to a fellow skydiver.

Relax

A floppy hand reminds a skydiver to breathe and stay calm.

COMPETITIVE SKYDIVING

The World Parachuting Championships takes place every two years.

Hundreds of athletes travel internationally to compete individually or as teams.

Judges award points for artistic movements during free fall, formation accuracy and precision in parachute steering.

78 Dancing for days...

could keep hunger at bay.

Today, elite athletes compete in dance competitions all around the world. They're judged on their choreography, technique and ability to execute complex moves. But in the 1920s, dancers across America competed in dance marathons judged on one thing only: **endurance**.

The craze taking the US by storm!

THE PEPPY STEPPERS

DANCE MARATHON

Rules:

Contestants must dance for 45 minutes every hour.

Contestants may sleep for 15 minutes each hour – beds provided on the dancefloor.*

If you stop moving, or your knees hit the floor, you're out.

The last couple dancing wins!

Marathon dancers have lasted

3,780 hours (157.5 days).

Do you have what it takes to beat that?

Free meals provided for all contestants! **

$500 CASH PRIZE ***

DISCLAIMERS:

* Contestants who fail to wake up after 15 minutes risk being plunged into ice water

** Contestants must continue dancing while they eat

*** As always, no guarantee that the organizers won't leave town before paying the prize money

79 The right laces...

win races.

For top athletes, every detail of a race, game or match can mean victory or defeat. Everything is considered to ensure they perform their best – right down to the laces on their shoes...

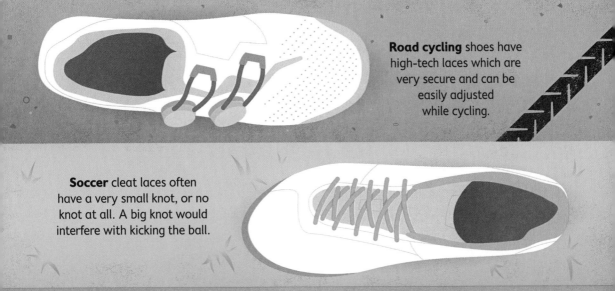

Road cycling shoes have high-tech laces which are very secure and can be easily adjusted while cycling.

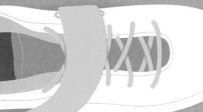

Soccer cleat laces often have a very small knot, or no knot at all. A big knot would interfere with kicking the ball.

Weightlifting shoes have a sturdy Velcro™ strap across the laces to keep the lifter's feet stable and supported.

In a triathlon an athlete swims, cycles and runs during a race. Trainers need to be pulled on quickly, so laces are made of stretchy elastic.

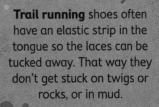

Trail running shoes often have an elastic strip in the tongue so the laces can be tucked away. That way they don't get stuck on twigs or rocks, or in mud.

80 Lost, found, stolen, replaced...

goes the story of the World Cup trophy.

The men's soccer World Cup trophy is one of the most famous awards in sports. You'd expect such a precious thing to be handled with extreme care. But that hasn't always been the case... Here are just *some* of the ups and downs the trophy has faced over the last 100 years.

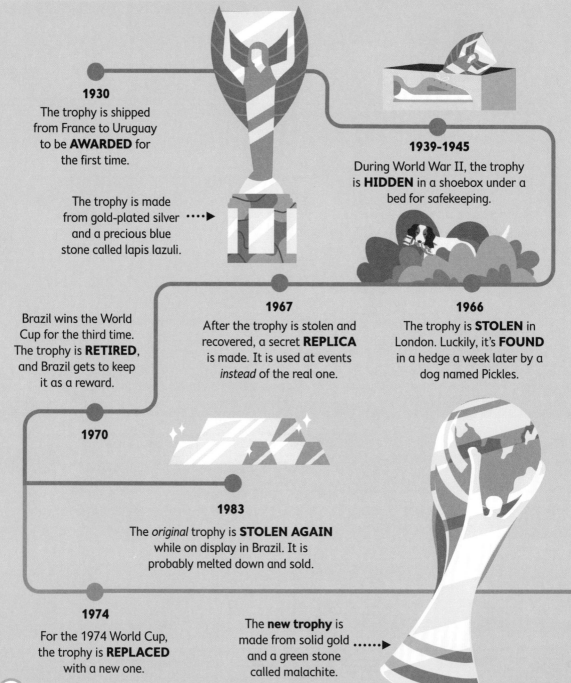

1930

The trophy is shipped from France to Uruguay to be **AWARDED** for the first time.

The trophy is made from gold-plated silver ····▶ and a precious blue stone called lapis lazuli.

1939-1945

During World War II, the trophy is **HIDDEN** in a shoebox under a bed for safekeeping.

1967

After the trophy is stolen and recovered, a secret **REPLICA** is made. It is used at events *instead* of the real one.

1966

The trophy is **STOLEN** in London. Luckily, it's **FOUND** in a hedge a week later by a dog named Pickles.

Brazil wins the World Cup for the third time. The trophy is **RETIRED**, and Brazil gets to keep it as a reward.

1970

1983

The *original* trophy is **STOLEN AGAIN** while on display in Brazil. It is probably melted down and sold.

1974

For the 1974 World Cup, the trophy is **REPLACED** with a new one.

The **new trophy** is made from solid gold ······▶ and a green stone called malachite.

SOCCER FACT FILE

Soccer is one of the most popular sports in the world.

It is played by
200 million
people in
200 countries
and followed by
3.5 billion
fans – that's almost half the people in the world!

Historians have found evidence of early forms of soccer in...

Ancient Greece,
2,400 years ago in 400BCE

Han dynasty, China,
2,300 years ago in 200-300BCE

Ancient Rome,
2,100 years ago in 100BCE

...as well as well-documented soccer-like games around the world, from French Guiana to Greenland.

The World Cup is the biggest international soccer competition, held every four years.
Each continent has its own major international competition too:

African Cup of Nations (Africa)

Asian Cup (Asia)

CONCACAF Gold Cup (North America, Central America and the Caribbean)

Copa América (South America)

European Championship (Europe)

OFC Nations Cup (Oceania)

The oldest soccer club in the world is Sheffield FC in England.
It has continuously been a soccer club since 1857 – over 150 years.

Today

Teams are no longer given the real trophy at all. They get a *replica* of the 1974 trophy. The real one is mostly kept in a locked vault in Zurich, Switzerland.

2042

The trophy will have to be **REPLACED** again, when the current trophy runs out of space for engraving the name of the winning team...

81 It took half a century...

for one marathon runner to finish his race.

In 1912, Japanese runner Shizo Kanakuri went to Sweden to compete in a marathon. Unfortunately, Kanakuri found that his race didn't go according to plan.

Weakened by the long journey and unusually hot weather, Kanakuri was already exhausted when he started the race.

Midway through the course, he pulled out of the event. But he didn't notify race officials who reported him as a missing person.

82 The darkness beyond the Sun...

makes a karate master.

Karate students progress through eight grades, called **kyu**, before they can become masters. At each stage, they wear a different colored belt. There are many interpretations of what the colors represent, but they're traditionally associated with the growth of a seed into a plant.

White belt
The beginning of a journey for a newly planted seed.

Yellow belt
The first beams of sunlight allow the seed to sprout.

Orange belt
The sunlight becomes stronger.

Green belt
The young plant produces more leaves.

RACE TIME:
54 YEARS, 8 MONTHS, 6 DAYS,
5 HOURS AND 32 MINUTES.

Blissfully unaware that he was being searched for, Kanakuri returned home to Japan to continue his training.

Fifty years later, Swedish officials discovered that Kanakuri was alive and well, so they invited him to complete his race — he crossed the finish line at the age of 75.

Not all karate schools include all of these belts in the same order.

Black belt

The black belt is reserved for a master of karate who has developed a deeper understanding of the art. It represents the darkness beyond the Sun.

Brown belt

The plant is mature and its seeds are ready for harvest.

Purple belt

A new day dawns on the plant.

Blue belt

The plant grows up toward the sky.

83 Cycling sideways...

helps track racers hit top speed.

Track cyclists race around an oval circuit known as a **velodrome**. Velodromes are specially designed with sloping tracks that help cyclists go extremely fast – as fast as cars.

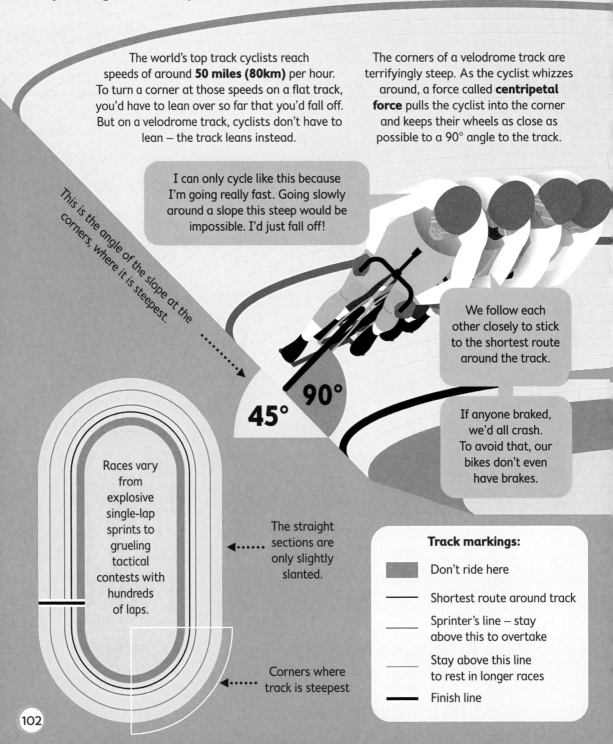

The world's top track cyclists reach speeds of around **50 miles (80km)** per hour. To turn a corner at those speeds on a flat track, you'd have to lean over so far that you'd fall off. But on a velodrome track, cyclists don't have to lean – the track leans instead.

The corners of a velodrome track are terrifyingly steep. As the cyclist whizzes around, a force called **centripetal force** pulls the cyclist into the corner and keeps their wheels as close as possible to a 90° angle to the track.

I can only cycle like this because I'm going really fast. Going slowly around a slope this steep would be impossible. I'd just fall off!

This is the angle of the slope at the corners, where it is steepest.

90°

45°

We follow each other closely to stick to the shortest route around the track.

If anyone braked, we'd all crash. To avoid that, our bikes don't even have brakes.

Races vary from explosive single-lap sprints to grueling tactical contests with hundreds of laps.

The straight sections are only slightly slanted.

Corners where track is steepest

Track markings:

Don't ride here

Shortest route around track

Sprinter's line – stay above this to overtake

Stay above this line to rest in longer races

Finish line

84 If your socks are too long...

you could be disqualified.

Sportswear can be so highly engineered it can give athletes an unfair advantage over their competitors – so there have to be rules. Here's an example...

Some cyclists wear long, tight socks called **compression socks**, which help their legs pump blood more efficiently. Use of these socks is strictly monitored.

BANNED CLOTHES

There are several sports where clothes that could give you an advantage are banned. **Running shoes** that are *too bouncy* and **swimsuits** that cut through the water *too quickly* have also been banned.

Your sock must come NO HIGHER than the mid-point between your ankle bone and knee bone.

I'm getting my ruler out to measure your socks, because they look suspiciously long.

A cyclist wearing socks that are too long can be fined, or even disqualified.

85 These pages are wider...

than a single scull rowing boat.

Racing rowing boats are light, long and narrow. This helps them to slice through the water as quickly as possible. The smallest of these boats, known as a **single scull**, is narrower than these pages opened out flat.

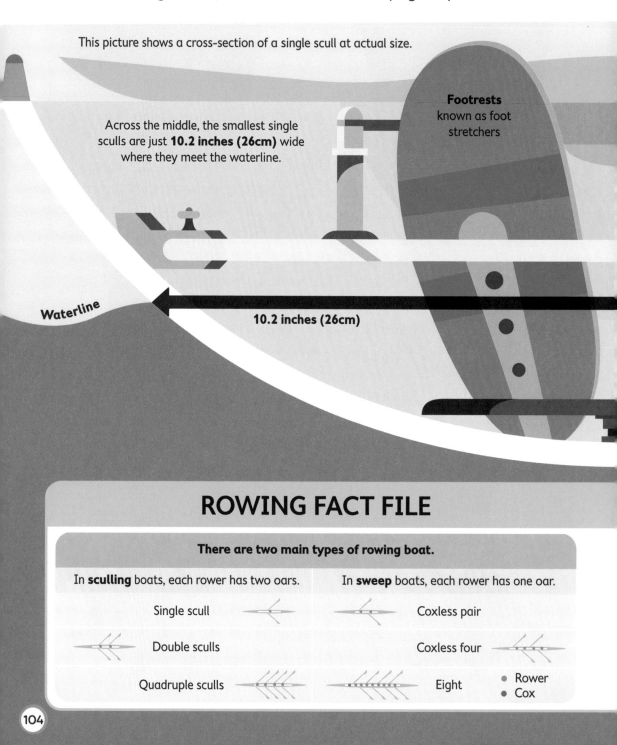

This picture shows a cross-section of a single scull at actual size.

Across the middle, the smallest single sculls are just **10.2 inches (26cm)** wide where they meet the waterline.

Footrests
known as foot stretchers

Waterline

10.2 inches (26cm)

ROWING FACT FILE

There are two main types of rowing boat.

In **sculling** boats, each rower has two oars. | In **sweep** boats, each rower has one oar.

Single scull	Coxless pair
Double sculls	Coxless four
Quadruple sculls	Eight

- Rower
- Cox

A single scull is rowed by one person with two oars.

Rowers always have their backs turned to the direction they're moving in.

Seat

Boats this narrow are speedy, but they're also very wobbly. If the rower rocks too much in their seat, the whole boat could tip over – so top rowers have to learn to row very smoothly.

The cox

In the eight, a crewmember called the **cox** faces the direction of travel and steers the boat.

Smaller boats can have a cox, but tend to be coxless in competition.

In coxless boats, one of the rowers controls the rudder using a wire attached to their foot.

Races

Most races are held on courses 1.2 miles (2km) long, no matter the size of the boat.

•••••• **Start Line**

Finish Line ••••••

Boats usually race side-by-side. Races can be one-on-one, or involve several boats separated into individual lanes.

86 One wheelchair...

turned into dozens.

The first parasport competitions were held in the 1940s. They involved just a few retired soldiers, all using conventional wheelchairs. But since then, engineers have developed a huge range of modified equipment and highly specialized wheelchairs for para athletes to compete in.

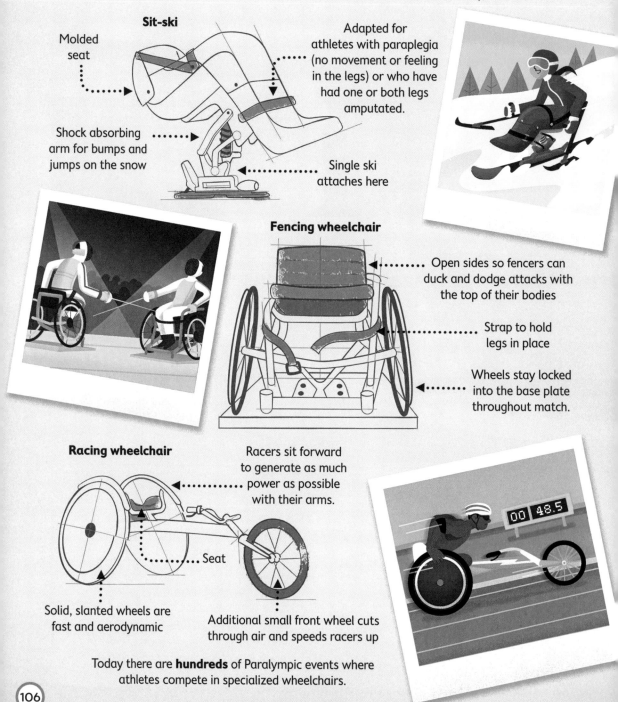

Sit-ski

Molded seat

Shock absorbing arm for bumps and jumps on the snow

Adapted for athletes with paraplegia (no movement or feeling in the legs) or who have had one or both legs amputated.

Single ski attaches here

Fencing wheelchair

Open sides so fencers can duck and dodge attacks with the top of their bodies

Strap to hold legs in place

Wheels stay locked into the base plate throughout match.

Racing wheelchair

Racers sit forward to generate as much power as possible with their arms.

Seat

Solid, slanted wheels are fast and aerodynamic

Additional small front wheel cuts through air and speeds racers up

00 48.5

Today there are **hundreds** of Paralympic events where athletes compete in specialized wheelchairs.

87 Discovering muddy footprints...

revealed an ancient athlete.

Professional sprinters rely on lightweight shoes, a bouncy track and years of training to do a 100m sprint in ten seconds or less. But archeologists studying ancient footprints think they have discovered a person who could run just as fast – barefoot – on slippery mud.

20,000 YEARS AGO

A hunter chased his prey across the wet mud of Australia's Gold Coast, leaving behind a trail of footprints.

The mud hardened and the footprints became fossilized in the ground.

THE YEAR 2003

The footprints were discovered. Archeologists team up with tracking experts to measure the hunter's trail. Their discovery was very unusual.

9ft (3m)

11 inches (29cm)

The hunter's stride was more than double his estimated body height.

His step frequency and foot position suggests he was running at an astonishing speed of 23 miles (37km) per hour, and was rapidly *accelerating*.

TODAY

Using this data, scientists estimate that the hunter could not only keep up with modern professional sprinters, but was also likely to be able to maintain his top speed for longer.

Shipwrecks on dry land...

drew fans to ancient Rome's most popular sport.

Chariot racing was hugely popular in ancient Rome. On race days, streets were deserted as Romans flocked to see flimsy horse-drawn carts hurtle around an oval track at dizzying speeds. The one thing they were all hoping to see? Spectacular, deadly crashes, known as *shipwrecks*.

NEIGH

CRASH

BANG

Lightweight wooden chariots were fast but shattered if they crashed, doing very little to protect the driver.

This driver is forcing a rival into the wall down the middle of the track.

ARGH!

This driver must cut himself free from the reins tangled around his waist.

Charioteers had to keep their guard up even when they weren't racing – rival teams sometimes tried to poison drivers and their horses.

EEK!

This driver must dodge galloping horses.

OW! This driver is whipping a competitor.

89 Magnificent riches...

awaited the best charioteers.

Many charioteers lost their lives on the track. But, if they survived and won races, they could attain riches so great that even the amounts paid to modern day soccer stars pale in comparison.

One charioteer, whose death-defying career spanned 4,257 races, including an incredible 1,462 wins, was named **Gaius Appuleius Diocles**.

Sum optimus!*

*I am the best!

Historians think Diocles's winnings over his lifetime were worth more than any modern sportsperson's earnings. He would have been one of the world's richest people today.

90 Champagne and rat poison...

kept marathon runners staggering on.

During long-distance races, runners battle hunger, thirst and exhaustion. So what's the best way to refuel an athlete and keep them on course? In the early 20th century, coaches had some *very* dangerous ideas...

During races in the 1900s, coaches gave their athletes special drinks to keep them going. Here are *some* of the ingredients they used in their recipes:

Brandy or cognac:
These strong wines contain lots of energy-giving sugar. But their high alcohol levels would have made athletes dizzy, clumsy and dehydrated.

Raw egg whites:
Along with energy and protein, which athletes need to grow muscles, these *could* contain bacteria that cause a fever, vomiting and cramps.

Champagne:
People thought the bubbles in this sparkling wine would revive a tired athlete.

Strychnine:
This deadly chemical was used in rat poison. It was thought to give athletes' bodies a jolt and fire up their muscles. But more than a tiny dose could kill them.

Suffering from the effects of their drinks, many early marathoners dropped out of races or had to be helped over the finish line.

Although scientists still disagree about their effectiveness, sports drinks are a booming global business.

91 Bump, set and spike...

to master the volleyball court.

In volleyball, two teams of six players take turns hitting a ball over a high net. A team scores a point if they make the ball hit the ground on the other team's side of the net. To make that happen, teams aim to pull off a carefully choreographed sequence of plays – the bump, set and spike.

Each team can touch the ball up to three times before hitting it back over the net.

Individual players must not touch the ball twice in a row.

1 THE BUMP

A pass played by hitting the ball with the forearms to a teammate positioned close to the net, known as the setter.

2 THE SET

The setter gently lifts the ball into the air with their fingertips. This move sets up the ball ready for one of the team's attacking players to strike.

3 THE SPIKE

An attacking player leaps high into the air and smashes the ball sharply downward into the opponent's court.

On the other side of the net, opposition players known as blockers scramble to prevent the ball from crossing the net. But a well executed spike is fiendishly difficult to stop.

Be a fighter and a dancer...
to dominate the capoeira circle.

This is the martial art of **capoeira**.
It originated in Brazil, but has spread around the world.
In capoeira competitors try to dominate the circle called the **roda**.

Dominating the roda involves filling as much space as possible...

...aiming powerful kicks...

...and scoring points for graceful, acrobatic moves.

This instrument is a **berimbao**. The faster it is played, the faster the fight.

Capoeira is so important to the culture of Brazil that it is protected by an organization called UNESCO. UNESCO looks after historical records of capoeira going back over 400 years. They also encourage people to participate in the sport, so that the tradition can continue for generations to come.

93 The wrong head...

sits on top of a sports sculpture.

One of the most iconic images of an athlete is a sculpture of a man throwing a discus. When archeologists found it in the 1700s, it was around a thousand years old. It was expertly carved out of marble. But there was just one small problem – its head was missing.

In order to sell the sculpture to wealthy collectors, an artist was tasked with restoring the statue.

The artist fixed it with a head that had supposedly been found near the statue...

...which was made from almost perfectly matched marble...

...so he put the pieces together in the way that *seemed* right to him.

Uh... I can't see what I'm doing.

Something's strange about that head!

Isn't it meant to *face* the discus?

Experts now agree that the head originally belonged to a different statue altogether, and that it definitely faces the wrong way.

Despite this, it has been preserved in its incorrect form, and it is on display at the British Museum.

Groovy tunes...

are the key to swimming success.

Swimmers often listen to music to motivate themselves before a race. But scientists think that a steady beat could be even more useful *in* the pool. A snappy rhythm has been shown to increase stroke rates and distance per stroke, helping swimmers move *faster* and *further* in training.

In fact, swimmers reported feeling less tired in the pool when listening to an upbeat tune than they did when swimming *without* music.

SWIM TRAINING *playlist*

1:05 ━━━━━━━━━━━━━ -2:33

Currently playing: **FREESTYLE FUNK** by the Front Crawlers

Scientists found that not just any upbeat song would do. Music that had between **120** and **140** beats per minute (BPM) produced the best results.

Studies have shown similar results for other sports too.
Cyclists benefited from music with **125-140 BPM**.
Runners found **120-130 BPM** worked best.

95 A long, hot shower...

awaits the winner of the Race Around the World.

At the Amundsen-Scott South Pole Station in Antarctica, hot water is in short supply. Residents are limited to a two-minute shower every few days. But there *is* a way to win yourself a longer, steamy, sudsy soak – by taking part in a special annual race.

Every year at Christmas time, a group of runners, cyclists and skiers compete in a race that loops around the South Pole.

Competitors may face sub-zero temperatures, freezing winds and snow... but not darkness. Christmas in Antarctica comes at the height of summer, when the Sun doesn't set, and it's light 24 hours a day.

The race is 2-3 miles (3-5km) long, and passes through every line of **longitude** – the imaginary lines that divide the globe from North to South on maps. And so the competition is known as the Race Around the World.

Sometimes, the lucky winner is awarded a rare and well-earned prize: a five-minute shower.

Logos on shirts...

make millions for sponsors.

Professional teams aren't just paid to play – they also get money for wearing brands and appearing in ads. This is called **sponsorship**, and though you might not always *notice* it, it's *everywhere*.

Regularly seeing brands and logos during games can make you more likely to buy something from those brands later on. Psychologists call this the **exposure effect**.

USB **2-0** RNE

Economists think that sponsors *make* at least 6 times more money than they *spend*. All because as you watch a sport, those little logos and ads get lodged in your memory.

In a single moment, on a single screen, these are just
some of the places where you might spot sponsorship:

Shirt sleeve	Shorts	The ball
Socks	Cleats	Around the field
Front of shirt	The stadium itself	Behind the officials
Back of shirt	Referees' jerseys	Up in the stands

Unconsciously, your brain links the player you admire, the team you support, or the excitement of the game with the brand you see.

In fact, the exposure effect works so well that companies are willing to shell out *millions* every year to have their logo displayed a during game — it's worth it.

97 A sporting handshake...

can be worth more than the outcome of the match.

Sports have the power to bring people together, break down barriers and start conversations. A simple handshake before or after a match has the power to change a lot more than just the game.

A MOMENT OF PEACE

Belgium, 1914

During World War I, troops from many countries faced each other in battle. But on Christmas Day, 1914, the gunfire fell silent.

Although they were on opposing sides in the War, for that one day British and German soldiers shook hands, exchanged gifts, sang carols together and played soccer.

A COUNTRY COMES TOGETHER

South Africa, 1995

For 50 years, people in South Africa were subject to apartheid – a system of racial segregation. Black people suffered, while many white people prospered. But in the early 1990s, apartheid ended and the country elected its first Black president – Nelson Mandela.

In 1995, the country hosted its first big event since apartheid ended: the Rugby Union World Cup. There was only one Black player for South Africa, and the country had a long way to go. But when Mandela presented the winning trophy to South Africa's captain, the country was briefly united in celebration.

98 The fastest runners...
get to race in the middle.

In track events, athletes all run the same distance, whichever lane they're in. But running in lane 1 isn't the same as running in lane 8.

A typical running track is a circuit, so the outside lane is longer than the inside lane. To even this out, runners in some races — such as 200m and 400m — have a staggered start, like this:

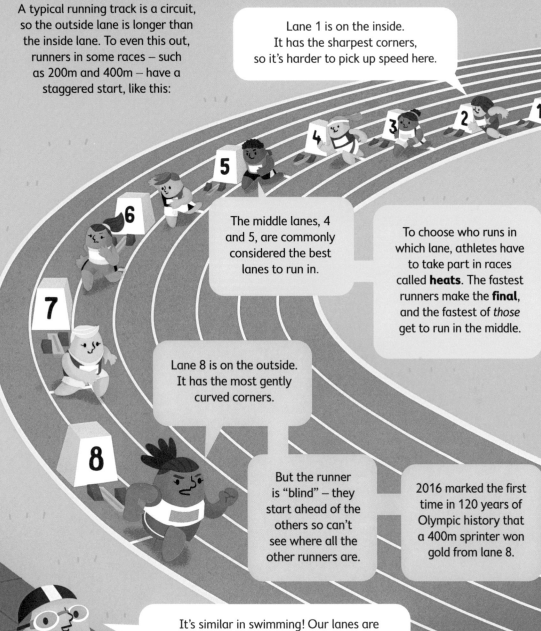

Lane 1 is on the inside. It has the sharpest corners, so it's harder to pick up speed here.

The middle lanes, 4 and 5, are commonly considered the best lanes to run in.

To choose who runs in which lane, athletes have to take part in races called **heats**. The fastest runners make the **final**, and the fastest of *those* get to run in the middle.

Lane 8 is on the outside. It has the most gently curved corners.

But the runner is "blind" — they start ahead of the others so can't see where all the other runners are.

2016 marked the first time in 120 years of Olympic history that a 400m sprinter won gold from lane 8.

It's similar in swimming! Our lanes are straight, but the outer lanes get really choppy during races. So the fastest qualifiers always swim in the middle lanes.

99 Making the final ascent...

is a record no one wants to set.

One of the top achievements in the sport of climbing is making a **first ascent** – being the *first* to climb a particular peak, rock face, or column of ice. But today, some climbers are setting records they never aimed for: being the *last* person to climb a route.

The reason for this is climate change. Temperatures around the world are rising, and the planet's high places are rapidly changing. In fact, some famous ice climbing routes are melting into thin air.

2000

2010

Here at the top of Mount Kilimanjaro in Tanzania, we climbers used to scale big towers of ice...

...but the mountain's famously snowy summit is in danger.

Between the years 2000 and 2010, **40%** of Kilimanjaro's ice disappeared.

2020

CLIMATE CHANGE AND SPORTS

Extreme weather caused by climate change continues to affect lots of other sports too.

Winter events, such as the 2023 Skiing World Cup and Para Snowboard Championships, were postponed due to a lack of snow.

The 2020 Tokyo Olympic marathon had to be relocated to a cooler city to reduce the risk of heat exhaustion.

To reduce the impact sports can have on our climate, engineers are working to invent energy-saving stadiums and sustainable equipment.

Scientists estimate that Mount Kilimanjaro will be completely ice-free by 2060.

A few years ago, I scaled a famous route up Kilimanjaro — but now there's not enough ice left to support a climber.

Unless we find a way to slow or reverse climate change, mine will probably go down in the record books as the final ascent.

100 When players retire...

their numbers can retire with them.

In many sports, players are identified by the numbers on their shirts. But players can't take *any* number they want. In some sports, when an iconic player retires, the club or league retires their number too, so no one else can wear it.

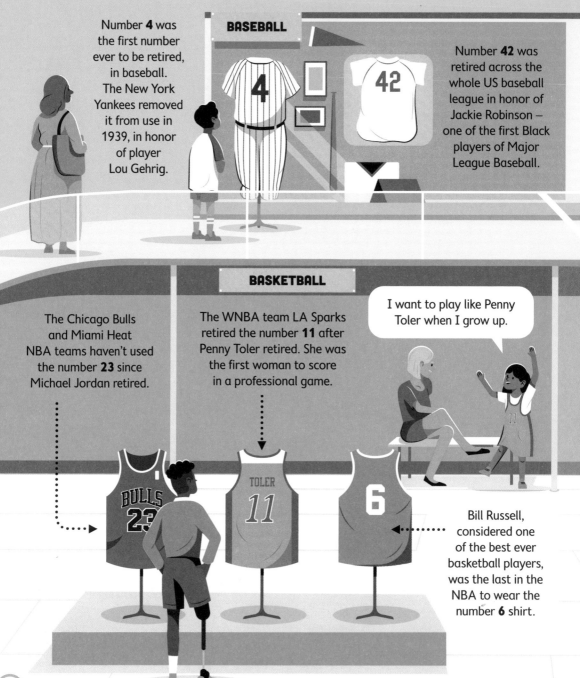

Number **4** was the first number ever to be retired, in baseball. The New York Yankees removed it from use in 1939, in honor of player Lou Gehrig.

BASEBALL

Number **42** was retired across the whole US baseball league in honor of Jackie Robinson — one of the first Black players of Major League Baseball.

BASKETBALL

The Chicago Bulls and Miami Heat NBA teams haven't used the number **23** since Michael Jordan retired.

The WNBA team LA Sparks retired the number **11** after Penny Toler retired. She was the first woman to score in a professional game.

I want to play like Penny Toler when I grow up.

BULLS 23

TOLER 11

6

Bill Russell, considered one of the best ever basketball players, was the last in the NBA to wear the number **6** shirt.

INFORMATION

In some sports, numbers tell you a player's position: **1** for a goalkeeper in soccer for example, or **2** for a hooker in rugby union.

In other sports, players can choose their own numbers, and often stick with a number throughout their careers.

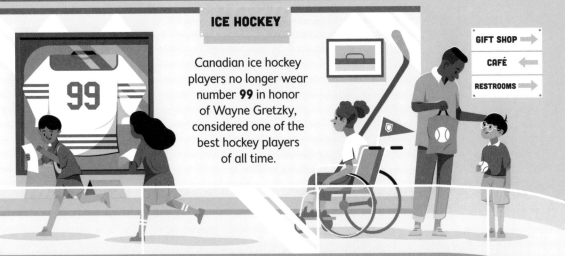

ICE HOCKEY

Canadian ice hockey players no longer wear number **99** in honor of Wayne Gretzky, considered one of the best hockey players of all time.

GIFT SHOP ➡

CAFÉ ⬅

RESTROOMS ➡

ROAD CYCLING

Road cyclists can be allocated different numbers for each race. Riders allocated number **13** often pin it upside-down, as the number is considered unlucky in some places.

SOCCER

In most friendly games, the Argentinian soccer team don't use the number **10**, in honor of player Diego Maradona. But they still have to play with it in official competitions.

Formula 1 drivers stopped racing with the number **17** on their cars, following the tragic crash and death of French racer Jules Bianchi.

FORMULA 1

Where on Earth?

The numbers on this map of the world show the locations of some of the "100 things" described in this book.

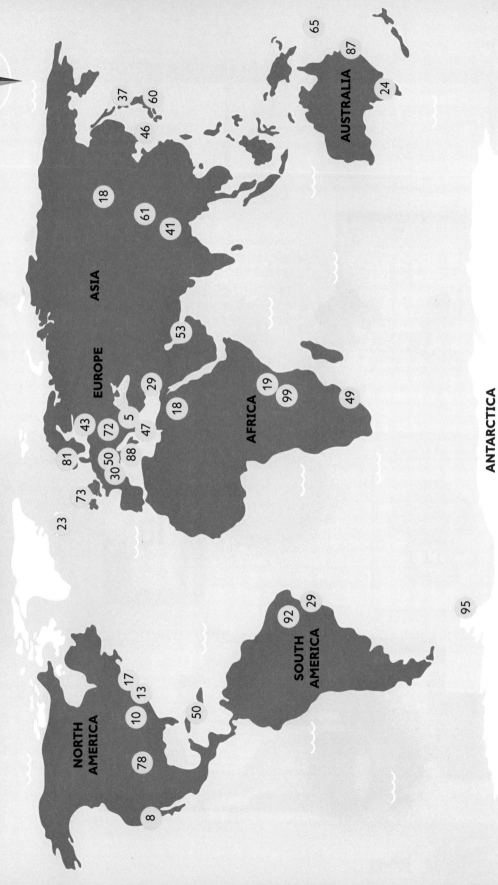

Index

It takes teamwork...
to finish a book of amazing sports facts.

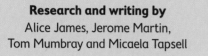

Research and writing by
Alice James, Jerome Martin,
Tom Mumbray and Micaela Tapsell

Designed by
Jenny Offley, Lenka Jones,
Lizzie Knott and Jenny Hastings

Additional designs by
Katie Miller

Illustrated by
Federico Mariani, Dominique Byron,
Parko Polo, Anton Hallmann
and Jake Williams

With expert advice from
Professor Martin Polley,
Dr. Romanda Dillon and
Show Racism the Red Card

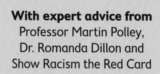

Series editor: Ruth Brocklehurst
Series designer: Helen Lee

First published in 2024 by Usborne Publishing Limited, 83-85 Saffron Hill, London EC1N 8RT, United Kingdom. usborne.com
Copyright © 2024 Usborne Publishing Limited. The name Usborne and the Balloon logo are registered trade marks of Usborne
Publishing Limited. All rights reserved. No part of this publication may be reproduced, stored in a retrieval system or transmitted
in any form or by any means without prior permission of the publisher. First published in America in 2024. AE